Open Your *Heart*

And Journal From Your Soul

DEB FRISCHMON

OPEN YOUR HEART
And Journal From Your Soul
By Deb Frischmon

Transcendent Publishing
P.O. Box 66202
St. Pete Beach, FL 33736
www.trancendentpublishing.com

ISBN: 978-1-7332773-5-8

Printed in the United States of America.

Dedication

To Tim,

Thank you for your love and never-ending support, encouraging me to follow my heart and live my dreams.

I'm so grateful for all the times you believed in me more than I believed in myself.

Love you now and forever!

"And I'd choose you, in a hundred lifetimes, in a hundred worlds, in any version of reality, I'd find you and I'd choose you."
-The Chaos of Stars

Acknowledgements

I am so grateful…

My deepest gratitude goes to all the people who have been reading my Open Your Heart, Mind and Soul Facebook and Instagram posts. I appreciate your support.

I am also so thankful for the supportive friends and family I have, who read my posts daily and have inspired me to keep going…

A special thanks to…

Chelle Anderson and Mary Nelson for taking such a strong interest in my work… supporting me daily and helping me publish this journal.

Laura Erdman-Luntz who was my yoga teacher trainer… who helped me "wake up"… inspiring me… helping me realize there is more in life.

Jim Herbert for being a sounding board… always helping me shift and evolve.

Jean Moore who supported me when I was creating my Open Your Heart page in 2016… who encouraged me to take a risk and put my message out there!

Xoxo

Introduction

About this journal…

Open Your Heart … And Journal From Your Soul is a journal created to spark you, light you up and open your heart, helping you to cultivate change and live your best life.

My personal self-discovery work and journaling started in 2010 when I became involved in a yoga teacher training program. During that time, I was hungry for new ideas and information. I had a deep longing to learn more about the REAL me. Throughout the process, it was as if a switch turned on inside me.

My soul was set on fire! I discovered there was a whole world out there that I didn't know existed, one that would ultimately change my life, changing my overall happiness.

On my journey, I experienced a huge shift of awareness regarding how I felt on the "inside." From the outside, I looked like I had the "perfect" life. I had a great job, an amazing husband, two wonderful boys and a beautiful home. I worked out and was healthy. We took regular vacations. I had wonderful friends and a close family. What more could I ask for?

On the inside, something wasn't right. I didn't feel content, connected, whole or complete. I engaged in a lot of negative self-talk that wasn't healthy for me. I lived in fear, spending most of my time regretting the past or fretting the future.

I worried about everything, especially if people liked me. I would waste a whole day worrying about something I had said to someone, only to find out later that they had never given it another thought.

Or, I would be anxious an entire week, wondering whether or not it was going to rain and disrupt an outside event or vacation. I couldn't wait to travel thinking it would make me happy once I was there, only to discover that while away, all I thought about was home.

I wish I could pinpoint what caused me to transform my old ways of thinking, and begin the process of being much more content and peaceful on the inside. Yet, I can't. After giving it a lot of thought, there are so many things.

I'm not claiming I have life figured out. It's far from that. What I've learned is life is a journey, and it will continue to be a journey, ebbing and flowing. Doing this work, life feels easier and more fulfilling each and every day.

I believe this journal will offer you guidance as I share some of the insights I've learned along the way. My intention is that you will read the quotes, read what I have written about them and get inspired to look at life differently. Then, go deeper into your life and soul, by taking time to reflect on the journal prompts and become aware of your thoughts and feelings.

The journal prompts are just ideas to get you started. You don't need to answer them all. You can write whatever comes up for you. You may not need prompts. Feel free to free write.

I invite you to "write from the heart," not trying to overthink by going into your mind. Set the intention to allow yourself to be curious and let it lead you wherever it goes. Let go of any need to be perfect and just play.

You can choose to go in order, or open the book up to a page and see what you need to know that day. Either way, it will be exactly what you need at that moment.

If you are like the "old" me, you probably won't want to journal right away, worrying someone might read it. However, I encourage you to give it a try. Take a chance on change and your own personal growth and transformation. You're worth it!

Over time, you will see how healing, empowering and life-changing it is to go deep into your soul, feeling your feelings, using your voice and doing what "lights you up."

When you put writing to paper, magic happens!

Let me know how it goes for you. I'd love to hear your story.

Happy journaling to you as you open your heart, mind and soul creating your BEST life!

Much love,

Deb

"I will be generous with my love today. I will sprinkle compliments and uplifting words everywhere I go. I will do this knowing that my words are like seeds and when they fall on fertile soul, a reflection of those seeds will grow into something greater."
-Steve Maraboli

It has been said that "We rise when we lift others…"
We all benefit when we are kinder to one another...
A little extra attention... goes along way...
We can consciously reach out... doing and saying nice things to our family...
friends... colleagues... neighbors...
Perhaps giving a compliment... saying some nice words...
Understanding a compliment can affect a person's day
or sometimes their whole life...
Affecting all of us... as it ripples out to the next person... and the next.
Today... Open your heart... taking time to make someone's day...
finding ways to lift them up...
Encourage them... saying kind words... finding the good in everyone...
it's always there!

Journaling from the soul…

How can you help others?
What are some compliments you could give others?
List all the ways you can bring the people in your life up.
Write a letter explaining how you want to help others and serve.

"And suddenly you know: It's time to start something new and trust in the magic of beginnings."

-Eckhart Tolle

When doors start to close... and life starts to shift...
and things don't feel stable...
We can recognize that it may be time to move on...
having faith and trusting... that we are being led...
Towards something new... towards something even better for us.
We can't create new... until we let go of the old... physically...
mentally... emotionally...
We cling tightly to what we have and know...
even when it doesn't serve us anymore...
We'd rather stay where it's familiar... than go towards something new...
towards the unknown...
We might worry about being "seen" as failing
when we end something...
Our perfectionist personalities fight to make the old work...
to "look" as if we are doing well.
It has been said... avoiding failure is to avoid progress.
Today... Consider that it may be time to make a change...
within your job... with a relationship... in your home...
with your love life... with the way you think... letting go of the old...
making room for the new.
Listening to your intuition... your inner wisdom...
your inner guidance system... it knows the way...
Trusting that it's natural to make changes in life...
as nothing stays the same...
knowing you have choices and being grateful you do.
Moving towards your dream life... making shifts... evolving...
creating the life you want to live!

Journaling from the soul…

What would a new chapter in your life look like?

"Happiness is not about the trophy or the finish line. It's the journey. If you can enjoy your journey, you can enjoy your life."
-Pharrell Williams

Sometimes... we get so focused on the finish line... we miss all the wonderful experiences and fun along the way... we miss living life.
Society teaches us to go... go... go... to achieve more... to obtain more... to be more... to want more... to do more...
that life should be a certain way.
And we get in the habit of chasing the next thing... continually focusing on the future... the next phase... "I'll be happy when..."
Not living or being in the moment...
not experiencing and enjoying the now...
There are people who wait their whole lives to be happy...
and it never comes.
Why are we waiting to be happy? Can we be happy right now?
Even if we perceive that life is not "perfect" or we have struggles?
Can we have goals... and dreams... and be content along the way...
that's when the magic happens!
Today... Slow down... breathe... smile... taking time to enjoy life... enjoying what you love to do... have fun spending quality time with the special people who are in your life... letting go of any rigid expectations you may have of how life "should" be...
Be happy with where you are today... being satisfied with where your loved ones are as well... being grateful... giving thanks...
loving and truly living life!

Journaling from the soul…

Where in your life are you not content?
Do you often wish for the future to be here?
When do you say, “I’ll be happy when…”?
What can you do right now to be happier with where you are today?

"Nothing ever goes away until it teaches us what we need to know."
~Pema Chodron

We all have situations that arise where we feel pain...
It's normal... it's life... things get better...
and then they may fall apart...
get better... and fall apart...
Life ebbs and flows...
As it does... we can grow and evolve... making room for this growth...
being aware... feeling our emotions... honoring them... and letting them pass...
healing the wounds in our bodies...
Learning from what life has to offer... going deeper... another layer...
Learning the lesson... so it doesn't present itself again... in a different situation...
different people involved...
Today... Breathe in deep... feel... feel your emotions...
be gentle with yourself... love yourself...
Do some mirror work... look into the mirror... look into your eyes... see your soul... your Higher Self... and say, "I love you"...
and notice what comes up... repeat... and take it in!

Journaling from the soul…

Where in your life do you find yourself experiencing the same lessons…
The same pain… again and again?
What have you learned so far?
After the mirror work… what did you experience?

"Everything comes to you at the right time.

Be patient."

-Unknown

It has been said that... patience is a virtue…
What does that mean?
It's when we wait for things to happen in their own time... naturally...
organically... Divinely timed...
In today's society... we live with a lot of instant gratification...
we are less patient...
We want things right now... struggling to trust and wait…
When we get impatient... it causes us to make quick decisions...
affecting our lives... our happiness... our overall joy.
How can we let go and trust the Universe?
One way is to embrace and celebrate the journey...
not only being happy when we reach the end point...
but being happy along the way.
We can also have more gratitude... being thankful for the small things...
attracting more to be thankful for... getting in the flow...
manifesting our desires.
Today... Slow down... trust... be patient if needed...
Believe what you want is on its way...
And when it arrives into your life... you will know it's right...
being grateful you were patient!

Journaling from the soul…

Where in your life are you not being patient?
How do you balance being patient and taking action?
What are you grateful for right now? Make a list…
Journal around what you desire as if it already has happened…

"The people who trigger us to feel negative emotions are messengers. They are messengers for the unhealed parts of our being."
-Teal Swanson

We all have areas to heal... we are human after all…
When we take responsibility for our own life... owning our feelings...
letting go of blaming... being a victim…
Our lives change rapidly…
When someone pushes our buttons and triggers us... it's helpful to look inside...
informing us... asking why did we attract this situation...
what do I need to heal...
When any uncomfortable feeling arises... we can name it...
"I feel angry"... "I feel hurt"... "I feel sad"... examine it... feel it... feeling what is in front of us... learning... transforming...
As we are willing to bring our awareness and attention to the center of the feeling… we can breathe into the feeling...
and then it can leave the body.
Today... Be aware of your feelings that come up...
notice what triggers you...
What is it trying to tell you? What might you need to heal?
For example... If someone criticizes you... and you get really mad and feel hurt...
maybe you are needing to heal the wound of...
"I'm not good enough." (Most of us have that wound...)
Breathe into the emotions that come up...
being grateful for the message...
if not in the moment... maybe later...
Helping you transform...
one day at a time!

Journaling from the soul…

Who triggers you? What is it telling you about yourself?
When do you get triggered?
Where does this come from? When did it first happen?
What emotion do you feel? What do you need to heal?

"Doing your best is more important than being the best."

~Zig Ziglar

In the inspiring book, The Four Agreements by Don Miguel Ruiz...
the fourth agreement is...
ALWAYS do your BEST...
Keeping in mind our best is never going to look the same
as someone else's.
Our best changes from one moment to another... morning or night...
sick or well... it ebbs and flows...
If we continually make "doing our best" a practice... our best will become better than it used to be.
As we work on doing our best... we need to be careful of trying too hard and doing more than our best... as that will eventually drain our energy...
And if we do less than our best... we feel guilty... frustrated...
have regrets... lowering our vibrations.
When we do our best... we learn to accept ourselves... learning life lessons when we make mistakes... being gentle with ourselves as we practice looking honestly at our actions... increasing our awareness...
When we do our best we take action... taking action is about living life...
without action we would not manifest what we want.
Today... Let go! Be gentler with yourself.
Try and be the best version of you... better than yesterday...
without overdoing it...
You are here to enjoy life... taking action... following the fun... ups and downs...
planting seeds...
creating your amazing future!

Journaling from the soul…

What does doing your best mean to you?
Do you go overboard and do MORE than your best? Overachieve?
Are you hard on yourself?
Name some ways you could have more fun in your life?

"Be an encourager. The world has plenty of critics already."
-Dave Willis

Be an encourager not a discourager…
Being someone who genuinely wants the best for others...
and celebrates when they do well... (letting go of jealousy... competition…)
Seeing the light in others... seeing that we are all the same...
we are all one…
Sometimes for someone to shift and change for the better...
all it takes is for them to receive kindness... love... support.
We can all reach out... helping others more...giving them hope...
inspiring them to be more... believing in them!
Today... Be generous with words you use…
Believe in others... everyone is doing the best they can…
Seeing their light... seeing their gifts... seeing their magnificence…
Trusting that kindness is the way... affecting one person...
affecting another...
eventually reaching out into the whole world!

Journaling from the soul…

How could you encourage others more?
Think of a time when someone encouraged you… how did it feel?
Are there people in your life who trigger you… where you feel jealousy?
Is it hard to encourage them?

"Disappointments are God's way of saying: "I've got something better, be patient, live life, have faith."

-Unknown

We all have experienced disappointments in our lives…
It's how we grow and evolve... and become the person who we
are meant to be.
We may try to avoid it by…
Playing it safe... not pushing ourselves... not living the life
we came here to live.
Or always overachieving... which may lead to burnout... exhaustion...
health problems…
We can learn to respond to disappointment in a healthy manner…
We can take a moment to honor our feelings and feel... feeling sad... hurt...
angry... whatever it is... not being embarrassed...
we all have moments like this.
We can ask... "Is this for our Higher good?"...
"Is it leading to something else that's better for us?"…
We can raise our vibe by turning to something that lights us up...
that makes us happy... leading to feeling better...
getting the ball rolling…
Today... Try and put whatever it is that you've been
"thinking about" into perspective...
Why is it happening? What can you learn from it?
Pray and ask God to help you see a new perspective...
Ask to have your fear-based thoughts healed…
using a prayer from the book…
<u>The Only Little Prayer you Need to Know</u>…
"God... please heal my fear-based thoughts"...
Creating miracles!

Journaling from the soul…

Have you had "bumps in the road" lately?
Do you believe they are for a reason? What have you learned?
Write a note from your Soul explaining the reasons.
Put the pen to the paper and just write… let it flow…

"When you do things from your soul,
you feel a river moving in you, a joy."
-Rumi

Connecting and operating more from our soul... less from our mind...
is important for our happiness.
When we do... we feel love... peace... joy... contentment…
How do we align and connect more with our souls?
We can… spend time in nature… journal daily sharing our true thoughts… spend time alone… pray… meditate… do yoga… go for a walk or run… try new things that take us out of our comfort zone… serve by doing things for others… do what we love to do… do nothing tuning into our senses… live in the moment...
breathe deeply...
Today... Make a commitment to start to connect and align with your Higher Self... being more conscious...
taking more time for you... the real you. Relax and feel…
Take a deep breath into your heart center... the center of your chest... expanding... opening... hold it... exhale audibly... with your mouth open... letting go... connecting... feeling better... repeat…

Journaling from the soul…

How do you connect with your inner self?
When you did the breath work… did you feel anything?
Write about times when you have connected more with your soul.

"Healing is an art. It takes time. It takes practice. It takes love."
-Maza-Dohta

Everything can heal in life.
We all have areas in our life that need healing... maybe physically... mentally... emotionally…
Louise Hay writes about how to love yourself and heal your life.
Her books are enlightening! I urge you to check her out if you haven't already.
She gives 10 ways we can love ourselves now and heal…

1. Stop all criticism
2. Forgive yourself
3. Let go of negative thinking
4. Be gentle with yourself
5. Be kind to yourself
6. Praise yourself
7. Support yourself
8. Take care of your body
9. Do things that bring you joy
10. Do mirror work-look into your eyes often-the windows of your soul... saying, "I love you" (try it... you may resist it at first... it's a little awkward... but so healing...)

Today... Ask to be healed...
Imagine yourself happy... whole... well…
Focus on what you want... not what you don't want…
Manifest great health by visualizing yourself well…
Know that when you heal... You help others as well!

Journaling from the soul…

What part of you needs to be healed?
Have a conversation with it… what does it say?
Why is it there? When did it first start?
What do you need to learn to get back in balance?
From the 10 ideas given… which one will you commit to trying?

"I will breathe.
I will think of solutions.
I will not let my worry control me.
I will not let my stress level break me.
I will simply breathe.
And it will be okay.
All is well."
-Shayne M.

We sometimes stress over things we can't control.
When we accept that we can't control everything in life...magic happens.
Taking positive action... doing our best... and letting go of the results.
When we let go of worrying about what potentially
"could go wrong"...
we create miracles.
It's been said most of what we worry about never happens...
and if it does happen... we are equipped to handle the outcome.
Today... Choose peace... peace of mind... freeing yourself...
Pray... asking for guidance... for comfort... reassurance...
Meditate... practicing mindfulness... focusing on your breathing...
Bring your awareness to your heart... breathing into your heart center for the count of 5... and out for 5... repeat...
Feeling love… gratitude… connecting with your Higher Self...
feeling calm... centered... reducing anxiety... stress...
Repeating the affirmation... "Today I let go... I am safe...
all is well... this too shall pass."

Journaling from the soul…

What do you worry about?
Have you noticed a pattern?
Write about what can "go right" in your life…

"Remember… The day you plant the seed is not the day you eat the fruit. Be patient. Be humble. Keep moving forward and know all this hard work you're putting in will produce the results you've been looking for. Your time is coming. Do not give up."

-Unknown

Sometimes we give up… right before the miracle is about to happen…
We all have dreams and desires...
waiting for them to come into fruition...
It's helpful when we let go of any doubt... as the more doubt we have...
the longer it will take.
It's important to believe... believing it can come our way...
We all deserve it…
Remembering... we weren't put on this earth to play it small…
Dreaming... and dreaming even bigger... why not?
Today... KNOW... you are worthy of great things…
Don't give up before your desires are manifested…
Keep taking action and doing the work...
and then letting go of the results...
believing you can live the life you dream about!
Affirmation for today...
"I am enough... I am worthy...
I am deserving of good things in life...
I allow miracles to enter my life..."

Journaling from the soul…

What seeds have you planted lately?
What are some signs they are coming to fruition?
What do you dream about happening… (dream big!)

"It will make sense one day. Your mission is to trust the process."
-The Universe

It's helpful to "trust the process" in life...
and let life unfold naturally…
Getting in the flow... connecting... to Source energy... believing…
Believing all is meant to be…
Letting go of control... opening our hands... letting go... letting God…
Being open to not knowing everything... embracing the unknown...
as we will never know all the answers here in the physical realm…
Expecting life to move on... healing... looking for the light...
continuing to follow what brings us joy.
Today... Trust in the process of life...
connecting with oneness... connecting with peace... joy... freedom... safety...
synchronicity... unconditional love...
Life is good!

Journaling from the soul…

What do you try to control in your life?
When you connect with Source… and get in the flow… how does it feel?
Write about a time (or create a future time) when you were flowing…
Or write a note to God explaining how you are going to let go and trust…

"Sometimes you have to stop worrying, wondering, and doubting. And have FAITH that things will work out, maybe not exactly how you planned, but just how it's meant to be."

-Unknown

We can be so hard on ourselves... stressing... overachieving...
Feeling disappointed when we don't "measure up"...
Measure up to what?
Measure up to our OWN personal standards and desired achievements...
Not meeting our rigid expectations...
We worry we aren't where we "think" we need to be right now...
"I should have been farther along by now..."
"I set goals last January... why haven't I achieved them?"
"What does it take to get ahead?"
"Will this ever work for me?"
What if we were meant to be exactly where we are right now...
and it's all in the plan...
Sometimes when we feel the dark... we appreciate the light so much...
We can always trust that our Higher Selves have been guiding us...
We can continue to listen even more... following...
being patient... it's coming!
In the meantime... we can have the practice of raising our vibration and keeping it up... doing what's best for us...
deciding to be happy and grateful right now.
Today... Have faith... trust...
Trust that good things are on the way for you!
It's your turn!

Journaling from the soul…

Do you have rigid expectations for yourself? Where does that come from?
Is anyone else holding you to these standards… or just you?
Do you have the same high expectations for others?
Write a note from your soul to "your human" reassuring that all is well.

"There is no passion to be found playing small, settling for a life that is less than the one you are capable of living."
-Nelson Mandela

Sometimes we just need to "jump"… and go forward.
Jumping... and building our wings on the way down... can be scary...
If we don't jump... we may miss amazing experiences
and chances in life...
Opportunities that were meant to be ours... ones we have manifested...
and asked for...
We might wonder if the risk is worth it... we may worry about building
our wings wrong...
The truth is... It might take more than one jump...
We jump... we fly... we may fall... we jump... we fly... we may fall...
We get the feeling of trying new things... succeeding... and love flying so much...
we build our wings again and again!
Today... Be open to Life's opportunities...
Go for it... take a risk... do what you have been wanting to do...
even if you don't feel ready...
It might not be easy at first... but it will be worth it...
Inhale... everything is going to be okay... exhale... letting go of fear...

Journaling from the soul…

Where in life do you play it small?
Where can you take more of a risk?
What would others say?
What does your soul want? Close your eyes and ask… wait… write…

"Observe your thoughts. Don't believe them."
-Eckhart Tolle

Many of our thoughts and beliefs we hold are not even ours...
Our minds come up with a lot of "stuff"...
Talking to us all day... "You should do this...
I can't believe you did that... He's terrible... She did this to me...
What will our future be like...
That was dumb... You're an idiot... I can't do it...
It will never work...
If only I had..."
All so unhealthy for us... holding us back from our true potential.
It's a helpful practice to become aware of our thoughts...
noting them... asking, "Is that even true?"
We can also ask the question... where am I coming from right now...
as we often come from lack... fear... competition... judgment...
Name it... acknowledge it... and release...
releasing the old limitation and habit.
Today... When your mind starts to talk negatively to you... notice it...
be aware... name it... release it...
And then breathe... connect with your Higher Self in your heart center...
in the now moment...
letting go of the past you regret or the future you fear...
Keep breathing deep... opening your heart...
knocking down the walls you may have created to protect...
building a bridge to Creator... to love...
to possibilities!

Journaling from the soul…

What have your thoughts been telling you lately?
Do you believe them?
Journal around something you have been hearing over and over.
What comes up? What does your inner self say?

"Fun fact: a lot of what weighs you down isn't yours to carry."
-Mel Robbins

We all know how it feels to care about others... and want to help them...
hoping and praying their lives become better.
We feel worried and have concern.
Which can be normal.
Is there a point where we take on too much?
When we let the troubles of others weigh us down...
Getting in the way of our own happiness... changing the quality of our lives.
The more "weight" we have... the longer we have to wait...
to manifest our dream life.
Today... Take time to think about how others affect you...
Do you take on the emotions and moods of other people?
Do you get caught up in the lives of others...
where it affects your day?
Do you make assumptions thinking the worst?
If so... it's time to take some time for yourself...
working on you...
getting some self-care... protecting your energy...
Honoring your needs and feelings...
Setting some healthy boundaries... loving you first...
and then when you're so full...
beaming out love and light to others!

Journaling from the soul…

How do others affect you?
Do you "carry" people? Do you feel others' feelings?
Where could you make changes in your life?
Make a list of ideas for self-care for you.

"Every situation in life is temporary. So, when life is good, make sure you enjoy and receive it fully. And when life is not good, remember that it will not last forever and better days are on the way."
-Jenny Young

We all worry... and have fear.
We sometimes get worked up... and stress out...
Life ebbs and flows...
Change happens...
Feelings come and go... feel them... honor them... and let them pass...
We can't always control what's happening externally...
but we can control how we react to it...
Remembering... the anxious thoughts we think... are just thoughts...
they aren't true... they're just thoughts... nothing else... be conscious...
notice them... and let them go.
Today... Stay calm... breathe... let go of any resistance...
letting go of fighting what's happening in your life...
Taking action towards what you want... surrendering...
allowing life to unfold naturally...
enjoying every moment of it!

Journaling from the soul…

What are you stressing over right now?
Is it even true?
How would you feel if you didn't have that worry?
What action can you take to make the situation better?
Write about what you can do… and how you will let go and let God.

"Go 24 hours without complaining, not even once. Then watch how your life starts to change."
-Katrina Mayer

It's a habit to complain about others and situations...
an unhealthy pattern... that's extremely draining for all.
When we complain we imply... we are right...
and someone else is wrong...
We may feel unconsciously better...
somehow feeling better about ourselves...
It might feel better in the moment...
but in the long run it doesn't serve us or anyone.
Today... Instead of finding fault with others...
focus on what you like in life... what you prefer...
shifting the pattern.
Letting go of judgment... fear... competition... lack...
All lower energies...
And watch your life change!

Journaling from the soul…

Do you have the habit of complaining?
About the weather… your job… your friends… your significant other…
If we judge others, we judge ourselves.
Write about how you judge yourself…
and where it might come from.

"Your soul is always going to whisper your truth back to you. Your soul wants what is best for you, and if you try to silence its voice, eventually the whisper will become a roar."
–Unknown

We are guided by our Higher Selves to do what we love to do...
and to live our best life...
But sometimes we don't pay attention.
We live in a world saying, "I should ..."
I should do this... I should do that... I should take that job...
I should be practical and settle for something I don't love...
Try not to "should" on yourself, and replace "I should"
with "I choose."
I choose to be grateful... I choose fun...
I choose inspiring situations and people to be around... I choose happiness...
I choose freedom...
I choose peace... I choose not to worry about what "might" happen...
I choose fulfillment... I choose passion... I choose to honor myself...
I choose to listen to my heart...
Today... Do what makes YOU happy...
choose to rise up… living a better life...
When you do... your soul will shine...
shining your light on the world...

Journaling from the soul…

What have you been hearing from your Inner Self?
Where in life do you do things because you think you "should."
Write about the changes you would like to make. Think big!

"Every morning we have two choices: continue to sleep with our dreams or continue to chase them."
-Carmelo Anthony

We dream about what we want in life... and then we have thoughts...
"That would never happen... That can't happen for me."
Maybe believing we are... too old... too late... not good enough...
not talented enough...
Perhaps believing there are too many others who are doing it...
there's not enough for everyone... living in scarcity and lack...
We can change our thinking... letting go of our limited beliefs...
releasing the voice in our head that convinces us
we can't have what we desire.
Remember… Anything is possible.
Today... When the voice in your head gives you a reason why
you can't do it or can't have something that you want...
Notice the feeling you have... feel it... release it... let it go...
Then try and imagine what can go right...
(close your eyes and visualize it...) then write it down...
Pen to the paper = magic!
Finally share it with someone...
taking one step at a time...
keeping your thoughts positive...
heading towards living your dreams!

Journaling from the soul…

What dreams do you have that you aren't pursuing?
What limited beliefs do you have that get in the way?
What feelings arise when you think about going after what you desire?
Visualize what can "go right"… and write about it!

"I'm realistic, I expect miracles."
-Wayne Dyer

Expect miracles!
We can experience more miracles in our lives by...
Being more open to them... believing in them... being more aware and connected to the Divine... meditating... praying... setting powerful intentions... living in the moment... being grateful...
loving ourselves and others unconditionally.
We need to ask for them... expect them... and watch what shows up...
not being attached to what we think the miracles "should" be.
A huge miracle can be a shift in our perception from fear
to love and acceptance.
Today... choose to have miracles in your life... never stop believing…
Take time to notice all of life's tiny miracles right in front of you...
when you do... magic will unfold all around you!

Journaling from the soul…

Do you believe in miracles?
List all the miracles in your life.
Set some powerful intentions by writing and declaring them.
Create a prayer giving gratitude in advance for what you want in life.

"Focus on not what others think of you... focus on adding value to the world... it's about your mission... not approval... it's about service... not popularity... your job is to stay on mission... regardless of the thoughts and actions of others..."

–Unknown

We might worry what everyone else might think about us...
We worry... and have fear... what if?
Worry is an old program that we have ingrained deep in our cells...
It gets in the way of truly being ourselves... being genuine... authentic...
It stops us from doing what we came here to do...
What if we let go of fear....
and let go of worrying what others might
think or say...
And we do what we want to do... doing what we came here to do...
doing what our heart desires!
Today... Where in your life are you holding back...
playing small?
Where do you have limited beliefs?
It's time to be bold... and take a few risks...
You might be surprised how good it feels to finally...
DO YOU!
Changing your life...
affecting the whole planet!
The time is NOW!

Journaling from the soul…

Where in your life do you play small?
Who do you worry is judging what you do?
What would you like to do that you haven't because of worry or fear?
Write yourself a letter from your future self thanking you
for taking risks and doing what you want to do.

"Self-confidence is the best outfit. Rock it and own it."
–Unknown

We spend too much time comparing ourselves to others…
Wishing we were something different.
Being confident is not always a natural skill…
luckily it's something we can practice and develop.
We can start with being aware of our thoughts and our self-talk…
Understanding… We have around 60,000 thoughts a day…
A lot are negative and fear-based…
and most of our thoughts are the same as the day before.
Our thoughts aren't always true…
so when we hear the negative chatter…
Let's pause… and change the radio station that plays in our head…
changing to a station that supports us.
Today… Embrace your confidence…
Why not think and believe... you're amazing… and unique…
and without you... the world wouldn't be the same!
Affirmation for today…
I approve of myself...
and I believe in me!

Journaling from the soul…

What is your self-confidence like?
What does the voice in your head say to you? Do you listen?
Do you compare yourself to others? Is it harmful to you?
Write a letter from your future self telling your now self
how you have changed…
explaining what you did… and how you feel…

"When you focus on problems, you will have more problems. When you focus on possibilities, you will have more opportunities."
-Unknown

What's your go-to? What do you focus on?
When we focus on our problems... it stresses us out...
and it gets in the way of taking positive action...
It gets in the way of connecting with our Higher Selves...
our intuition... lowering our energy...
leading us to feel stuck and blocked...
Can we train ourselves to look for the good...
and possibly look at our problems as opportunities...
Opportunities to shift... learn... grow... evolve...
This takes practice to "train the brain..."
Living in acceptance... understanding we all have problems that will arise...
we will continually ebb and flow...
surrendering to what is...
Finding the gift... when something happens that we don't like...
looking for the new improvement... the learning...
the new potential...
Today... Focus on what matters...
Focus on all the infinite possibilities...
Shifting... creating opportunities!
Breathe into your heart center... (hope... positivity… and light...)
Hold for two seconds...
Breathe out (fear... worry… and anything you need to let go of...)
allowing it to dissolve...
Feeling more peace and joy!

Journaling from the soul…

What is your go-to? Do you focus on what could go wrong or possibilities?
Write about what you want to happen in your life…
Read it to someone.
Create a vision board showing what you desire…
Displaying it where you will see it every day.

"The way we choose to see the world creates the world we see."

-Barry Kaufman

We can train our minds to see life differently...
Looking at life in a negative manner doesn't get us anywhere...
we just attract more negativity.
When we look at life that way... we live in lack...
we notice what's missing in our lives...
we don't believe that we can have an abundant life...
When we look at life with different eyes... we see so much more...
we see all that life has to offer... witnessing awe and miracles...
we believe in an abundant world...
remembering we have the power
to co-create our best life.
There's no "coincidence" that people who live a great life...
practice being cheerful and happy.
We have a choice... and hopefully we choose to live life to the fullest...
with optimism... with purpose... being curious and open...
expecting the best and finding good in all.
Today... "Change the way you look at things...
and the things you look at will change." -Wayne Dyer
When you notice yourself finding what's wrong...
let's say the weather... your family... or your work...
you can change your outlook...
Breaking the habit of complaining...
Turning it around and naming what is positive...
what you are grateful for... giving thanks...
changing your life!

Journaling from the soul…

Think about where you complain in your life.
Then turn it around… and change the way you look at it…
list it… and write all the positives… list what you're grateful for…
Write an appreciation letter to someone.
(Send it if you feel it's appropriate.)

"Learn to accept people for who they are,
not who you want them to be."
-Unknown

Acceptance is an important key in life... of ourselves... and others...
When we have "expectations" of how someone "should" behave... we go into judgment of them... which has a low vibration and causes separation.
They can feel that energy... and it ripples...
How can we be more accepting... more loving?
It starts with ourselves... if we love ourselves unconditionally... we will love others.
Instead of trying to change others... we can work on us.
Maybe examining our personal expectations of ourselves...
We can watch our thoughts... being aware of when we start to judge...
Noticing and naming our judgment... without judging ourselves.
Today... Awareness is key... notice your thoughts... your feelings... notice if you are operating from lack... frustration... irritation... disappointment... anger...
Breathe into those feelings... ask to feel love and acceptance instead... feeling love and acceptance in your heart center... opening the heart... feeling love... sending the world love!

Journaling from the soul…

Where does your judgement come from?
How can you be more accepting… more loving?
How can you add more self-love into your life?
What are some ways you could be more grateful?

"Talk about your blessings more than you talk about your burdens."
-Unknown

It's helpful to focus on what we want... not on what we don't want.
We get what we think about... whether we want it or not...
As we focus and look for what's positive in our day...
and consciously find the blessings... we can give thanks...
with much gratitude.
Being grateful for the little things that we take for granted
in our lives...
Hot water... a roof over our head... safety... choices... free will...
When we have extreme gratitude for what we already have
and even for what we don't have YET...
we raise our vibration... we get into the flow...
we attract high vibrational circumstances into our lives...
and miracles happen.
Today... Recognize your blessings... give thanks...
make a list mentally in your head... speak them out loud...
write them down...
When you do...
watch your whole life turn around!

Journaling from the soul…

Do you have a hard time focusing on the positive?
What are you thankful for? Make a list.
Write a gratitude letter.

"Follow your bliss and the universe will open doors where there were only walls."
-Joseph Campbell

We have all built walls around ourselves...
We may think it is to protect us... but unfortunately...
it doesn't serve us well...
It cuts us off from Life... from Source... from Flow...
When we build these walls... we create separation... pain... suffering...
Rather than union... connection... wholeness... oneness...
It's time to knock these walls down... one brick at a time.
Today... Contemplate...
Where in your life have you created a wall
that needs to be taken down...
a place where you can build a bridge in its place...
Connecting... uncovering... being authentic and genuine...
being real...
Taking the mask off...
being you.

Journaling from the soul…

Do you protect your heart?
Do you know what you are passionate about?
Do you take time to do what you love to do?
Write about you opening your heart and following your bliss!

"If we really want to live, we must learn how to forgive."
-Mother Teresa

Forgiveness is powerful. It can change our lives.
Sometimes we don't even know we are holding on to negative thoughts and energy... or still holding a grudge.
Sometimes we are unaware that we need to forgive...
ourselves... others...
It's buried deep...
We might realize it when our bodies start to speak to us...
with chronic pain...
When we forgive... we can release this negative energy...
and let it go... helping us thrive in life.
Forgiveness needs to be a practice.
The practice might include… journal work...
Writing a letter and not sending it... EFT tapping... prayer... meditation...
Ancient Hawaiian prayer Ho'oponopono-
"I love you... I'm sorry... please forgive me... thank you."
When we practice forgiveness... we develop a skill...
leading to mastery... becoming automatic...
Freeing us from emotional and mental weight...
the stuff that holds us back in life... keeping us stuck...
repeating the same pattern over and over.
Today... Be aware... forgive... yourself... others...
make it your practice... set yourself free...
not only just surviving in life...
but thriving!

Journaling from the soul…

Where in your life do you need to practice forgiveness?
With yourself? Others? Both?
Write a letter to someone who you need to forgive.
Tear it up… burn it… or send it if you feel it's beneficial.

"Anything that annoys you is teaching you patience. Anyone who abandons you is teaching you how to stand up on your own two feet. Anything that angers you is teaching you forgiveness and compassion. Anything that has power over you is teaching you how to take your power back. Anything that you hate is teaching you unconditional love. Anything you fear is teaching you courage to overcome your fear. Anything you can't control is teaching you how to let go and trust the Universe."

-Jack Kiddard

Life teaches us so much… we just have to be willing to learn.
We all have feelings and emotions that don't feel good at times...
creating discomfort.
It's helpful if we drop the label of "good" or "bad"...
And just being aware and curious.
Emotions are God's gift to us... to be used as a guidance system...
giving us information... so we can learn... and change...
They are E-Motions... energy in motion... letting them move on!
Today... Pay attention to your emotions... noticing the ones that keep showing up... informing you of what's going on inside.
Take a deep breath in… breathing into the feeling and feel...
exhale... letting go of resisting...
Take another deep breath in... feeling love... peace...
and safety in your heart... exhaling releasing... letting go!
Loving and appreciating your life!

Journaling from the soul…

Who triggers you? (Where you get a charged emotion)
What emotions keep showing up for you?
Write about them and how they make you feel.
Telling where you feel them.
Close your eyes… feel the emotion… allow it to pass.
Then go to your heart center… what emotion do you want to feel?
Ask your Higher Self to help you feel that new emotion in your heart.

"The energy that you put out... comes back to you."
-Eckhart Tolle

The law of cause and effect... also known as karma...
is a powerful law of the universe.
It's like a boomerang... what you throw out... comes back.
If you throw out anything negative... negativity will come back.
If you throw out anything positive... you will receive positivity.
You get what you give...
So if you want support... give support.
If you want love... give love.
If you want respect... give respect.
Today... Put out some positive vibes...
sending out what you want back...
Being mindful of your thoughts... words... and actions...
and watch your life change!

Journaling from the soul…

What do you usually put out into the universe?
What kind of thoughts do you have?
What kind of words do you say?
Write about your "future life"… exaggerate… dream big… feel it!

"Don't fall back into your old patterns of living just because they're more comfortable and easier to access. Remember, you left certain habits and situations behind for a reason: to improve your life. And right now, you can't move forward if you keep going back."
-Marcandangel

Making positive changes in our lives and moving towards the life we desire is a practice... it most likely won't happen overnight.
We have had years of conditioning... thinking... programming...
We can be more gentle with ourselves... as we "unwind"...
"reprogram"... and "reboot"...
Connecting with the present moment... and tuning into how we feel...
being aware of the emotions that arise...
feeling the discomfort without judgement.
Getting quiet and meditating... "finding our calm"... relieving anxiety... grounding ourselves... connecting with Mother Earth...
breathing deeply... relaxing.
Today... Notice when you start to go back to the old...
where it may feel temporarily safe and more comfortable...
Being aware... being more conscious...
paying attention to the voice in your head...
Setting the intention to go forward... towards the new...
towards the life you have been waiting for!

Journaling from the soul…

Where in your life are you trying to change?
Tell how you find yourself going back to the familiar.
How does that serve you?
Write about what you want in life…
and notice if what you struggle to "let go" fits in with your new vision.

"The goal of meditation isn't to control your thoughts,

it's to stop letting them control you."

-Unknown

Our thoughts create our lives... we attract what we think...
believe... feel...
We all have the power to change our thoughts...
When our minds are racing... it's a sign for us to know we feel separate...
and it's time to connect with Source... by slowing down...
getting quiet... meditating.
A lot of people say meditation is hard... they say they are not good at it...
or it doesn't feel right... or they worry they are doing it wrong...
Just know... there's no wrong way. There is no bad meditation.
Meditation is a practice we can cultivate... it takes time and commitment...
Just like getting in shape at the gym... we wouldn't go a few times and expect major results...
Sometimes we think meditation is sitting in silence in lotus pose...
very still for a long time... (old way of thinking)
Meditation can happen anywhere... can be anything...
and look different for everyone...
Keeping your awareness on your inhale and your exhale... letting your thoughts go... (they won't completely go away... if you have a thought... notice it... try not to judge it... and go back to following your breath.)
Inhale... open your heart... exhale... feel love and gratitude...
Try that for 5 minutes a day... until it feels comfortable... then 10...
and so on...
There are so many more benefits from meditating regularly...
We connect with our Higher Selves... we sleep better... we reduce stress... anger...
we improve clarity and performance... we feel peaceful and calm!
Today... Slow down... take time for you... try not to look at meditation as a chore... or something you have to do...
Meditate to connect... to turn to love... clearing your mind...
living a happier life!

Journaling from the soul…

Do you have thoughts that keep your mind racing… spinning…?
Do you sometimes feel alone… separate?
Close your eyes for 5 minutes… focus on your breath…
Inhale... open your heart... exhale... feel love and gratitude…
Open your eyes and write what you saw… felt… heard… know…

"Never believe you are above anyone or below anyone.
Keep a humble spirit."
-Brandon Burchard

We are all on a journey… we are not better than others…
and others are not better than us.
We are all human... on our own journeys... learning in life...
experiencing highs and lows....
We can choose to see others as being the same...
as we are all one...
not feeling better or less than...
Being more humble in life... being kind to all... lifting others up...
As we all need more love... encouragement... support…
inspiration… care...
Today...
Live your life trying to be a better person than you were yesterday...
letting go of judgment...
Staying in your own lane... not comparing...
Helping others when needed... lifting everyone up...
living a wonderful life!

Journaling from the soul…

Are you a humble person?
Where could you be more humble?
Do you compare yourself to others… thinking they are better?
How can you be a better person than you were yesterday?

"Follow your heart and intuition.
They know what's truly best for you."
-Unknown

We are here to live life... taking chances... changing our minds... shifting... growing... evolving... without judgement...
None of us have all the answers... we can't control life.
There are so many unknowns in our world... and that's what makes life so fun... amazing... mystical...
We can embrace and trust in the unknown...
not having to know every outcome...
Having faith... trusting that our intuition... the still small voice inside...
our God spark... is always leading and guiding us...
If it "feels" good... not just in the moment... but in the long run... we know we are on the right path... and we can continue... if it doesn't "feel" right... we will know.
Not letting fear get in our way... (F.E.A.R... False Evidence Appearing Real)
Today... Slow down... tune into what your heart is telling you...
it's always leading you... let love be your guide...
Believing that good things are not only possible... but are on the way....
leading to a happy and fulfilling life!

Journaling from the soul…

Do you have a hard time embracing the unknown?
What has your heart been telling you lately?
Write a letter from your Higher Self to your human self.

"I am not what happens to me. I am what I choose to become."
-Carl Jung

It has been said… that our life is OUR story…
and we need to write well and edit often…
We are not our past...
Our past does not define us…
We are not our circumstances…
We've all had hardship and we've all made mistakes...
Every day is a gift...
A chance for a new beginning… to start over…
creating the life we want to live...
Creating a new story… a story worth living…
a story where we forgive ourselves and others...
making the best of the life we have here on planet earth.
Today… Rewrite your story... and let go...
Letting go of judging yourself for your past…
you are not the same person you once were…
Letting go of judging or blaming anyone else for your life…
taking responsibility...
Learning from your past… your circumstances…
any mistakes that have been made...
And then let it go… focusing on the present…
what you can do now…
what you want to do...
what you can do for others!
The future is so bright!

Journaling from the soul…

What is your story?
What do you tell people?
How would you like to change your life?
Rewrite your story.

"Everything you want is on the other side of fear."

-Jack Canfield

Fear is an emotion we feel... sometimes for a good reason...
as it may help and guide us..
Unfortunately... most of the time... it gets in our way...
preventing us from living the life we want to live.
Sometimes we have negative thoughts that come to us...
telling us why we should quit and give up...
why things won't work...
why we aren't good enough... why others are better than us...
These are just thoughts... that aren't even true...
we've created them ourselves... perhaps using assumptions...
When we have these fearful thoughts... it's an indicator we have disconnected from Source... and we are out of balance...
and need to go back.
To create more clarity... peace... and harmony...
We can cultivate a daily practice of... meditating... going within... praying...
spending time in nature... getting enough sleep...
using moderation with food and drinks... saying no more.
Today... Make it a practice to take care of you...
creating your best life.
Notice when you are having thoughts that aren't serving you...
taking the time to go within and connect...
making choices that make you feel good.
Inhale into your heart center for the count of 5...
opening your heart... hold for the count of 2... exhale from your heart center for the count of 5… and as you exhale… picture a flower blooming in that area…

Repeat.

Journaling from the soul…

Where do you have fear in your life?
What are you afraid of happening?
How do you take care of yourself?
Create a list… listing ways to take care of you…
Title it… "Extreme Self-Care List."

"Always show more kindness than seems necessary, because the person receiving it needs it more than you will ever know."
-Unknown

We all feel better when people are kind.
If someone is not being kind... deep down they are probably hurting themselves...
so it's helpful to be kind to them.
When we are kind to others... we increase our own happiness...
As what goes around comes around...
When we are kind to others... it ripples out into the world...
it's contagious... and kindness always comes back...
Today... Stay humble... choose kindness...
letting go of having to be "right"...
you will feel better about situations.
Do something for yourself taking care of you...
as well as others...
it will create joy... happiness...
brightening up the world!

Journaling from the soul...

Do you have the habit of having to be "right?"
Where does that come from?
Make a list of everything you can do today
that will help kindness ripple out into the world.

"Let go of comparing where you're at with where everyone else is. It doesn't move you farther ahead, improve your situation, or help you find peace. It just feeds your shame, fuels your feelings of inadequacy, and ultimately it keeps you stuck."

-Danielle Koepke

We would be happier if we stop comparing ourselves to others.
Comparing ourselves to others is a habit...
that doesn't serve us very well.
We are all here doing different things...
we have different goals and dreams...
with unique ideas and experiences.
It's been said... comparison is the thief of joy. So true.
When we compare... it literally sucks the joy
right out of our present experience...
and future experiences.
When we compare ourselves to others... we feel bad...
we lower our vibration... attracting lower vibrational circumstances...
people, things, and events into our lives.
Today... Let go of comparing...
it's an unhealthy habit that gets in the way...
Reminding yourself that you are enough... you have enough...
the grass is not greener...
Loving your life... where you are right now...
enjoying your sacred journey...
every step of the way!

Journaling from the soul...

When do you compare yourself to others?
Does it get in the way of your happiness?
If you asked others, what are your gifts and strengths...
what would they say?
Focus on that!

"It helps if you remember that everyone is doing their best from their level of consciousness."
-Deepak Chopra

We can all assume everyone is doing the best that they can.
Everyone's consciousness is different based on their makeup
and their experiences in life.
We have no idea what someone else is thinking... what they have been through...
or what they are going through right now.
We can only see life through our eyes... our experiences... our perspective...
our level of consciousness...
Which isn't "right"... it's just what we know... and believe to be true.
We are not better.
Can we try harder to understand others...
giving them the benefit of the doubt...
Letting go of criticizing... Letting go of judgement...
Letting go of resentment and anger... that's just fear we're feeling...
It can be toxic... effecting the mind... body... and spirit...
When we make this shift... the world shifts... as we are all one.
Today... Forgive others... love one another... being kind...
letting go of finding faults... giving people the benefit of the doubt...
See everyone's light... as we are all light...
Open your heart... mind... and soul...
Reach out to someone who needs it today...
letting them know you care!

Journaling from the soul…

Who do you judge and get frustrated with for their behavior?
Where in your life have you done the best you could…
yet others may have seen it differently?
Write about forgiving others and allowing them to be
who they are right now.

"If I've learned anything in life...
It's that sometimes, the darkest times can bring us to the brightest places. I've learned that the most toxic people can teach us the most important lessons; that our most painful struggles can grant us the most necessary growth; and that the most heartbreaking losses of friendship and love can make room for the most wonderful people. I've learned that what seems like a curse in the moment can actually be a blessing, and that what seems like the end of the road is actually just the discovery that we are meant to travel down a different path."
-Daniell Koepke

We have all had endings in our life… some easier than others.
Our lives continue to change... and we are sometimes forced to shift, grow, and move forward.
When we resist these changes... it will only hurt us in the long run.
Resisting... puts up blocks... holds us back.
What we resist... persists.
When we are open and allow... we raise our vibrations...
letting in and attracting the new and better.
Today... Understand life will continue to shift... letting go and trusting...
new doors will open.
Keep moving forward... starting a new chapter in your life...
the beginning of a new and great adventure!

Journaling from the soul…

What are you resisting right now?
Are you in a dark place? Have you been there before?
Write about a hardship you are going through or have gone through.
What is the gift from that situation? Or past situations?

"When the world says... give up. Hope whispers... keep going."
-Unknown

Miracles happen every day.
When we believe in miracles... anything is possible…
We sometimes want to give up on... our dreams... people... our jobs...
our relationships... our health and wellness…
It helps to focus on what we want.... our desired end result...
rather than what we don't want…
Taking time to visualize and dream about the way we want it to be...
rather than focusing on what's not going well…
Saying a few prayers... asking for guidance and help... asking to see a different perspective or to have our fear-based thoughts healed.
Today... Keep believing... having hope... expecting miracles…
People and situations change every day…
Believing that something beautiful is going to happen...
and the best is yet to come!

Journaling from the soul…

Miracles happen every day…
What miracles have happened in your life?
What do you desire in life?
Journal around that… (And then focus on it…)

"Tell everyone you know...
My happiness depends on me... so you're off the hook.
And then demonstrate it.
Be content and happy no matter what anyone else is doing.
Practice feeling good... no matter what.
And before you know it... you will not give anyone responsibility
for the way you feel."
-Abraham Hicks

Our happiness depends on ourselves.
When we rely on others or outside circumstances to be happy...
we always end up disappointed... We give our power away.
Today... Let go of depending on other people and certain conditions
for your happiness...
Happiness is an inside job...
Cultivate a practice where you feel good as much as you can...
by doing the things you love to do... choose what you say yes to wisely...
being grateful for all you have!
Enjoying your life right now!
Affirmation for today... "I love my life... I am blessed..."

Journaling from the soul…

Are you happy most of the time?
Do you work on yourself… loving yourself… taking care of yourself?
Do you rely on others and outside circumstances to make you happy?
What can you do to be even happier? Make a plan.

"When you hold grudges, your hands aren't free to catch blessings."
-Unknown

Hanging on to grudges... hurts everyone...
It takes strength and character to forgive... let go... and move on...
creating peace... being more compassionate...
Being willing to look at and understand both sides...
As there are always two sides to every story....
Today... Open your heart... let go of stubbornness... bitterness... giving others the benefit of the doubt... remembering everyone is trying to do the best they can... creating peace... love... joy... and harmony!

Journaling from the soul…

Do you hold grudges? If so… for what? Towards who?
If you forgive others easily… do you forgive yourself too?
Do you need to forgive others more?
Write about the hardest moment in your life…
Change the ending if needed… writing about how you Let go and Let God!

"Take no offense. That which offends you only weakens you. Being offended creates the same destructive energy that offended you in the first place. Transcend your ego and stay in peace."

-Wayne Dyer

When we are continually offended... it's a sign that tells us there's something going on... within ourselves...
When we are offended... we experience low emotions.... fear... doubt... worry... anger... blame... revenge... hatred... rage...
We give our power away...
We give power to negative energy that comes our way...
and therefore we create and attract more of it...
When we feel offended... we close our hearts... not letting Source energy flow through us...
When we start to feel this way... we can be aware... training ourselves to see others as doing the best they can... and keep our hearts open.
We can own our part in what's happening...
We can also take care of us... knowing that when we have a higher vibration... we are more resilient... loving.. compassionate...
We can get more sleep... eat better... hydrate more...
move our bodies...
let go and have fun... pray... meditate... get outside...
Today... Be strong... get grounded... cultivate peace and love within...
making it your practice to slow down... breathe...
connect with the Divine... Source energy...
Eventually letting any negativity that comes your way... not stick...
like Teflon... not getting affected...
shine bright!

Journaling from the soul…

When have you felt offended in the past?
Do you give your power away by letting others control how you feel?
How can you shift these feelings?
Write how the "new you" will be stronger… grounded… more centered.

"You can't go back and change the beginning, but you can start where you are and change the ending."
-C.S. Lewis

We all have the power to… change our lives... heal our pasts…
change our stories.
It takes conscious work and practice.
If we mainly focus on our past... our mishaps... what happened...
who did what... who hurt us... whose fault it is...
we stay trapped and stuck... and we create more of that same story.
People are a mirror to us and they mirror back what's inside.
What we can do is move on... shift our energy...
focusing on what we want in life... imagining the life we want to live...
Starting to see the people in our lives differently... giving them a chance...
believing they can change as we continually do.
Today... Take your power back... creating the life you want to live.
Maybe creating or updating your dream board
indicating what you want in life.
As our thoughts create our reality...
Journal often about your dream life. It's okay to dream...
and don't forget to dream big.
We live in a magical universe with miracles happening every day!
Believe!

Journaling from the soul…

What do you dream about happening in your life?
Journal… sharing what you desire in all areas of your life.
(Set the timer for five minutes and write from the heart
without over-thinking.)
Create a dream board illustrating your desires.

"Never compare your journey with someone else's. Your journey is your journey not a competition."
-Unknown

Competing... comparing... and having to be the best...
can be destructive.
When we compare... we enjoy nothing...
it brings up lower vibrational emotions such as envy... anger... depression...
feeling bad about ourselves.
Which doesn't help us go further in life... instead it slows down our progress and maybe even prevents dreams from coming true.
When we give up the need to win... being in ego mode...
wanting to prove others wrong...
And we let go of measuring our value and worth by how we stack up against others... Our lives will start to change...
And everything will magically start to fall into place!
Today... Give up the need to be the best...
bringing more peace into your life.
If you're going to compare... compare yourself
with who you were yesterday...
Becoming happier and more successful every day!

Journaling from the soul…

Who do you compare yourself to? Who triggers you?
Where in life are you trying to be "the best"?
How can you shift that old pattern?
Write about ways you can "let go."

"Every time I judge someone else, I reveal
an unhealed part of myself."
-Shawn Duperson

When we judge others... it shows we are the ones hurting inside.
The people we judge offer a mirror to us... showing us our fears...
our shadow sides that we bury deep...
For example if we judge someone for not looking a certain way...
it may indicate we have our own fears and insecurities around
the way we look.
Or we judge other's behavior... which shows we worry about
and regret our own behaviors...
We avoid our own "stuff" and unknowingly project it onto others.
We do that when we gossip about others as well.
Judgement keeps us separate... stuck... unhappy...
It lowers our vibe and we attract lower vibrational people... situations...
and events into our lives.
Today... Take note of when you judge others or situations whether in your head
or out loud…
Without judgment of yourself!
Being gentle and kind towards yourself... it's just a defensive habit you have
developed that can be dissolved...
Honoring the hidden wound you discover as you become more aware...
Shifting... becoming free... healing... being more kind...
living a better life!

Journaling from the soul…

Do you judge others? Yourself?
What do you judge about yourself?
What do you judge about others?
Reflect on any hidden wounds you have that might cause you to judge others.

"It doesn't matter how slowly you go as long as you do not stop."
-Confucius

Sometimes we are hard on ourselves believing we aren't making enough progress... we might feel stuck.
What we don't realize is the beauty of how far we have come in life... recognizing and appreciating all our personal growth and experiences that have shaped us to be who we are today.
Our dreams and purpose in life are constantly changing and evolving... shifting as we experience more and more.
What we once desired perhaps is not the same...
so we may slow down to reassess.
Or we come up against a "bump in the road" giving us time to think.
Sometimes we simply need a gentle rest on our journeys... to heal...
to nurture ourselves.
Whatever it is... we can honor it... as we slowly keep going...
finding the joy and magic along the way!
Today... Don't give up... your dreams are on their way...
continue to believe...
ALL IS WELL... trusting in the Divine timing in life and letting go.
You are exactly where you are meant to be!

Journaling from the soul…

Do you feel stuck?
Are you experiencing any "bumps in the road" lately or maybe in the past?
Where have you been in the past? List all the positives!
Where do you want to go?
Create "baby" steps for you to take towards your desire.

"You yourself, as much as anybody in the entire universe, deserves your love and affection."
-Buddha

Loving ourselves is a practice we can cultivate...
It might feel foreign to us... as we may have been taught to think about others before ourselves. How can we love ourselves more?
We can start by healing from the inside out... healing old wounds...
old thought patterns... letting negative emotions we have stuffed deep down…
come to the surface... (regret... guilt... shame... anger... hatred...)
feeling and honoring them... letting them go...
Accepting ourselves is crucial for self-love. Letting go of being our own biggest critic... it's time to let that go! Being aware when we criticize ourselves...
and say, "STOP!"
Take time to appreciate ourselves... writing in our journals all we love and appreciate about ourselves... and if we can do that...
we will be able to do it authentically for others…
without feeling judgement or competition.
Today... Take time to love you...
the most important relationship you can have... it's not too late!
And when you do... you will attract people with a higher vibration into your life who love themselves too... who will also love you!
"In order to truly love others... you must first love yourself!"

Journaling from the soul…

How can you love yourself more?
What do you need to let go?
What can you add to enhance your life?
List everything you love about yourself.

"One person's energetic shift has the power to create a ripple effect around the world."
-Gabby Bernstein

We are all one... all interconnected...
It has been said... we are collectively like a pond...
and our souls are like the drops in the pond...
If someone would skip a rock into the pond...
Only a few drops would be touched...
But the pond... as a whole...
Would experience it as well...
What we do to ourselves... and what we do to others...
we do to all... on some level.
We all can be part of creating a POSITIVE ripple effect.
We can all make a difference in the world... shifting our planet...
We can change our energy... our vibration... going from fear to love...
Love vibrates the highest... as well as passion... excitement... joy...
freedom... appreciation...
We can do kind deeds for others... impacting them...
We can be conscious of our words...
as our words have power and energy...
We can give to others... our time... our attention... our love... money.
Today... Focus on what you can do for the world...
changing your attitude... mindset... your energy.
Consciously change your vibe...
the more positive energy you put out...
the more we all get back...
And with an open heart...
being kind and generous to all...
rippling out into the world...
changing one life at a time.

Journaling from the soul…

Do you believe we are all connected?
Do you think your actions affect others in the world?
How can you increase your vibration… your energy?
What can you do to change yourself… ultimately changing the world?

"Never wait for the perfect moment.
Just take a moment and make it perfect."
-Unknown

A lot of us have rigid expectations in life.
Expectations in our relationships... our jobs... our experiences...
Sometimes it is difficult to let go of these expectations
because we've had them for a very long time...
Having expectations that are too high...
expecting too much from ourselves and others.
Being so hard on ourselves and others when we don't meet them.
Learning to let go of these expectations takes practice...
and takes acceptance of what is... loving what is.
Today... Appreciate where you are right now...
and what you have.
Being grateful for all your blessings and gifts...
loving yourself and others...
while aspiring for a brighter future.
And as you do... you raise your vibration...
attracting more of what you want in life...
creating your best life!

Journaling from the soul…

Do you have rigid expectations?
Do you have a hard time accepting life as it is?
What do you want in life?
What are you grateful for right now?

"Just as birds are meant to soar, so are you, meant to dream."
-The Universe

It's important to dream... and then dream even bigger.
When we know what we want in life... we can focus on that...
attracting it into our lives.
We must have the courage to put it out there... and then pursue it...
taking a small action... and then another...
While believing it can happen... continuing to picture what we want...
not what we don't want...
Letting go of living in fear mode... letting go of believing dreams are for other people... believing they don't come true.
Today... Think about what you want in life.
Start to journal around your dream life...
putting it out into the Universe...
Having fun creating...
Not forgetting to dream big...
believing dreams come true!

Journaling from the soul…

Dream about your "dream" life!
List categories… (job… home… family… significant other… friends… travel…)
Then write without giving it much thought…
Letting the dreams come from the heart!

"Surrender to what is, let go of what was, have faith in what will be."
-Sonia Ricotti

We can all surrender... and then surrender some more.
When we think about surrendering... we may think it means...
to give up.
It actually means something very different from that.
When we surrender... we let go of wasting our energy fighting...
resisting what is...
And we relax and accept where we are in life... right here...
right now...
It may not be perfect...
It may feel uncomfortable...
And when we accept... we get out of fight or flight mode...
we start to heal... moving towards what we want in life.
Today... Let go... and let God... surrendering...
to a force greater than you.
Being lighter... being kinder with yourself... (when we are kinder with ourselves we are kinder to others)... not beating yourself up for things you have done... or not done...
Forgiving yourself... being yourself...
laughing at yourself when needed...
Having the attitude of... I'm okay...
I'm okay where I am right now... working towards what I want...
I'm doing the best I can... I can relax... I have enough time...
all is well!

Journaling from the soul…

Where can you surrender more in life?
Are you a perfectionist?
Do you try and control everything and everyone?
Name ways you can be kinder to yourself…
Set some intentions.

"Working hard is important. But there is something that matters even more: BELIEVING in YOURSELF."
-Harry Potter

When we believe in ourselves... all else falls into place...
We attract what we want in life... and all the right people and right situations present themselves to us.
Sometimes we don't even know that we've lost faith in ourselves...
it happens slowly along our journey...
Unaware that our self-esteem has lowered...
not valuing ourselves as much as we used to.
Perhaps we lost faith in ourselves... when we experienced a setback...
or when we were rejected... disappointed...
or maybe we made a mistake...
We can become aware... searching for the gift or lesson in the situation...
getting back up... moving on...
Accepting where we are... and believing we have the capability to do whatever we want to do...
Getting clear on what we really want...
putting it out into the Universe...
Focusing on that desire... not focusing on what we don't want... as we get what we focus on whether we want it or not...
It's helpful to think about how we manifested our past successes.
Then take some action... surrendering and letting go... trusting...
all will be well!
Today... Believe in you... if you don't... who will?
You owe it to yourself...
You are way more capable and worthy than you know...
you are a powerful spiritual being...
with the power to create your best life...
you've got this!

Journaling from the soul…

Who do you personally know who whole-heartedly believes in themselves?
What traits do they have that you desire?
What changes can you make to believe in yourself more?
Write a letter to yourself from your future self
thanking you for making changes.

"When you are grateful, fear disappears and abundance appears."
-Tony Robbins

A true state of gratitude... is being aware... and deeply appreciating...
all the miracles in our lives.
When we are grateful... we raise our vibration...
and connect with Source Energy... the longer we stay in gratitude...
the stronger the connection...
When our vibrations are that high...
we attract higher vibrational people... things... and events into our lives...
When we are grateful... we send out positive energy...
and positive energy comes back to us...
When we are struggling to be grateful...
we can finish the following sentences...
That was good because...
I am grateful for...
I'm so blessed because...
I love...
Today... Find gratitude in your life...
looking for the small miracles that are all around you...
rather than finding what's wrong... (it's just a habit...)
Being grateful is a practice to develop and work on...
one beautiful moment at a time!

Journaling from the soul…

Finish the following sentences...

That was good because...

I am grateful for...

I'm so blessed because...

I love...

"Grace... is meeting those moments on the journey, then picking yourself back up, being humble enough to learn, and not being too hard on yourself."
-Michelle Peluso

Hard times often lead to great things.
We all make mistakes... and live an imperfect life.
We are all working on being a better person than we were yesterday.
When things don't go the way we'd like... we can learn...
grow... evolve...
We can be kinder with ourselves... more gentle...
letting go of punishing ourselves...
Letting go of holding onto lower energies that weaken us...
such as regret... guilt... shame... blame... hatred...
Today... Forgive yourself...
Letting go of perfection... being okay with making mistakes... failing...
getting back up again... being stronger.
Knowing that everything in life offers us the opportunity to change...
shift... transform...
creating a great life!

Journaling from the soul…

Do you feel regret for anything?
Do you feel guilt for past events or anything in your life right now?
Do you blame anyone for what has happened in your life?
Do you feel anger towards others or situations?
All perfectly normal to feel… name it… write about it… feel it… let it go!

"Everything works out in your favor once you take care of yourself. Hydrate, stretch, sleep enough, connect with your lover, eat healthy food, and take care of your mind and body, no matter what."
-Unknown

We seem to be busier than ever...
Let's not forgot about the most important thing...
Taking care of us.
Just like the oxygen mask on an airplane...
we cannot help others if we don't help ourselves first.
When we put ourselves first… all else falls into place.
Today... Where in your life could you make a change?
Write it down... tell someone and ask them to hold you accountable...
Do you need more sleep? More water? Do you need to move your body?
Eat healthier? Drink less?
Do you need to say no to others or something... saying yes to you?
Whatever it is... pick one thing...
Let's not try to boil the ocean... one habit at a time...
Changing your life...
because you're worth it!!!

Journaling from the soul…

Where in your life could you make a change? (Tell someone!)
Do you say yes to others… saying no to you?
Write about how you're going to change that story…
Create a new story for yourself… dream and write…

"Don't chase love, money, or success. Become the best version of yourself and those things will chase you."
-Tony Gaskins

There's many benefits to living the best version of ourselves...
When we do...
Life starts getting easier... we get into a flow... feeling connected...
feeling inspired... synchronicities come into our lives again and again...
and we heal and attract greatness!
We inspire others to do the same... and the people around us...
and people afar... suddenly start to shift and change for the better...
we don't even have to say a word... we just need to embody it...
living it...
How do we become the best version of ourselves?
There are so many ways... here are a few...
-Showing up fully each and every day...
-Being present (the past is over... the future will come...
live in the moment)
-Taking care of our bodies (home of our soul)
-Owning it... owning and loving who we are today… (Just do YOU!)
-Letting go... letting go of hardships... worry... resentment... fear... control...
judgment... (especially of ourselves...)
-Doing what we love... having passions... living life on purpose.
-Having fun!
Today... Work towards being the best version of you!
When you do... all you want in life will follow...
Living the life you dream about living!

Journaling from the soul…

How can you become the best version of you?
What can you add into your daily practice?
Name it… write about it…
explaining how you will shift and change your life!

"Don't wait for things to get better. Life will always be complicated.
Learn to be happy right now, otherwise you'll run out of time."
-Tiny Buddha

There was a doctor who moved to the US to work at the
Mayo Clinic in MN...
He claims he wasn't happy before he came and thought he would be happy when
he moved and lived in America.
That didn't happen. And then he noticed others
weren't very happy either.
So he did research and conducted a study on happiness...
and found humans are not wired to be automatically happy.
Our brains are not hard-wired for contentment...
Happiness needs to be cultivated... and made a habit...
a constant conscious effort...
Knowing this... we can be more gentle with ourselves when
we aren't feeling it.
We can understand there are a lot of people feeling the same way...
And we can consciously start to shift our vibration...
doing what lights us up...
It might take work... and practice...
Perhaps...
Meditating... connecting with the God spark within...
Breathing deep... calming the nervous system and mind...
Appreciating life... there's so much to be grateful for...
Smiling more... when we smile we release serotonin...
Hanging out with people who lift you up... we all have choice...
Letting go more... letting go of rigid expectations
leading to more ease and pleasure.
Today... Change your life... start developing your happy habits...
perhaps make a list of what lights you up...
And then do those!
Each and every day!

Journaling from the soul…

Do you resonate with the story
about the doctor who realized we aren't programmed to be happy?
What do you do in your life to make happiness a practice?
List all the "happy habits" you want to add to your life.

"Promote what you love instead of bashing what you hate."
-Zig Ziglar

Our focus is so powerful...
Do we use our words to empower... encourage... motivate... build up...
or to tear down...
Do we talk about our blessings more than our burdens...
Do we focus on what we love... rather than focusing on what we don't...
finding fault in everything...
When we focus on what we don't love... we get more of that...
Where our attention goes... our energy flows.
Today... Start to shift your attention to what you want in life...
Love... peace... harmony... joy... compassion... gratitude... ease...
And watch your world change!

Journaling from the soul…

What is your main focus in life?
Do you promote what you love?
Look back at any social media sites you have…
what message do you send out?
Write about all you want to focus on in your life.

"Listen to the silence. It has so much to say."

-Rumi

We can all work on silencing our minds.
If we don't... we will feel exhausted.
We wake up in the morning and our minds go right to anything that was negative from the day before... rather than thinking about all the good. (Tell it to stop... and immediately go to what you appreciate in life...)
We stand in front of the mirror and our mind starts to find all our perceived faults... not being very nice... (tell it to be grateful... being grateful for the body that has housed your soul for all these years... aging gracefully...)
Throughout the day... our inner dialogue may not support us...
comparing ourselves to others... telling ourselves we aren't good enough...
(don't listen... it's not true...)
We fall asleep happy and satisfied with our day...
and then we wake up in the middle of the night... worried... anxious...
thinking about our problems... (breathe in slowly for 5 counts...
into the heart... hold it for 2...
exhale for 5... repeat... connecting...)
Today... Quiet the mental chatter... by slowing down...
remembering you are the one observing...
Being mindful...
Connecting with Source in your heart center... opening your heart...
feeling safe... protected... loved...
awakening your soul!

Journaling from the soul…

When you wake up… what do you hear inside your head?
When you look in the mirror… what do you say to yourself?
How do you quiet your mind?
Close your eyes and breathe… follow your inhale and exhale…
Notice what arises… Open your eyes… write about it.

"You will know your path by the fun of it."
-Abraham Hicks

Following our passions and purpose in life is so important.
We all have a unique purpose if not many purposes...
Our purpose is always evolving and changing...
it's important to stay open...
When we live our life on purpose... and fall in love with life...
we feel alive... matching our own innermost being.
When that happens... everything falls into place... doors open...
the right people and right circumstances show up at the right time...
What are you naturally drawn to?
What do you love to do? What makes your heart sing?
What would you do if you knew you wouldn't fail? Be bold!
Put it out there!
Today... Follow the passion and fun... following what you love...
what lights you up... when you do... magic happens...
Leading to doing what you love to do... potentially everyday...
making others happy too...
Continuing to follow your heart... as it knows the way...
living a fulfilling life...
one day at a time!

Journaling from the soul…

Are you doing what you love to do in this life?
If you are doing what you love to do… how does it make you feel?
What makes your heart sing?
Dream and write about how life could be fun and easy. Dream big!

"If we learn to open our hearts, anyone, including the people who drive us crazy, can be our teacher."

-Pema Chodron

When we are more compassionate… life is better.
We can all practice being more compassionate...
being more tolerant... more grateful... more open.
Even towards the ones who "push our buttons."
Allowing moments of irritation... to give us information...
Informing us of what's going on "inside" of us...
as life mirrors back what's inside of us...
Wounds we haven't healed... insecurities... our fears...
old habits and patterns... our shadow sides....
Today... Open your heart... and mind...
being more compassionate to all.
Think about the people who you will be in contact with today... tomorrow...
or later this week...
How can you show them more compassion?
More appreciation?
Changing your life...
changing the lives of others!

Journaling from the soul…

Who pushes your buttons?
Who can you show more compassion towards?
What can you do?
Make a list of all the good deeds you can do for others.

"Everything you blame, you're stuck with. Bless it. Wish it well. Wish it its own freedom, and it will be very powerful in the way that it will not come back to you. If you don't forgive it, if you don't bless it, if you don't wish it well, the energy will just be magically drawn back to you because it's looking for resolution. All negative energy that we've inherited, is there because it's looking for resolution."

-Adyashanti

Forgiveness changes everything.
Sometimes it's not so easy to forgive... to forgive others...
to forgive ourselves...
We may not feel ready...
We can lean into the hurt... the pain... the loss... the resentment...
the disappointment... and feel it... allowing it to bubble up...
Accepting it... accepting that it did happen... not pushing it away...
And eventually letting it pass through us... letting go...
Not allowing it to hold us back anymore...
Moving forward...
Not letting what happened to us in the past...
affect the life we live now.
Today... Work towards forgiving... others... yourself...
It's time to set yourself free...
Life is too short and precious...
make it your best...
it's never too late!

Journaling from the soul…

Who do you blame?
How can you bless the situation?
How can you forgive more?
Write a letter to yourself or someone else forgiving them.

"Health is not just what you eat. It is also what you think and say."
-Unknown

It's important to pay attention to our whole beings...
mind... body... spirit...
We focus on our physical bodies... focusing on what we eat and drink...
how much exercise we get... which is important.
Unfortunately, we might neglect to pay attention to the rest of us...
One area we neglect is being aware of our thoughts...
Our thoughts are so important... as they can create what
happens in our lives...
We often have thoughts that don't serve us...
Cutting us down... hindering our motivation... believing the world is out to get
us... finding what's wrong with everyone and everything (including ourselves)...
filling us full of worry... fear... dread...
leading to a life we don't enjoy.
Today... Notice and become aware when you are having negative thoughts or
speaking negative words...
(all old programs and habits...)
Stop... and counter them with something more positive...
shifting your energy... shifting the collective energy of the planet.

Journaling from the soul…

Write about your wellness.
What do you do to take care of yourself?
Where do you need a little more attention?
Write a letter from your future self thanking you for the changes you have made.

"Note to self: It's time to let go."
–Unknown

We all want to surrender more and let go. And we may ask... HOW!?
Reverend Safire Rose explains it beautifully...
"She/He let go. Without a thought or a word, she let go.
She let go of the fear. She let go of the judgments.
She let go of the confluence of opinions swarming around her head.
She let go of the committee of indecision within her. She let go of all the 'right' reasons. Wholly and completely, without hesitation or worry, she just let go.
She didn't ask anyone for advice. She didn't read a book on how to let go. She didn't search the scriptures. She just let go.
She let go of all of the memories that held her back.
She let go of all of the anxiety that kept her from moving forward.
She let go of the planning and all of the calculations about
how to do it just right.
She didn't promise to let go. She didn't journal about it. She didn't write the projected date in her Day-Timer. She made no public announcement and put no ad in the paper. She didn't check the weather report or read her daily horoscope.
She just let go.
She didn't analyze whether she should let go. She didn't call her friends to discuss the matter. She didn't do a five-step Spiritual Mind Treatment.
She didn't call the prayer line. She didn't utter one word. She just let go.
No one was around when it happened. There was no applause or congratulations.
No one thanked her or praised her. No one noticed a thing.
Like a leaf falling from a tree, she just let go.
There was no effort. There was no struggle. It wasn't good and it wasn't bad.
It was what it was, and it is just that.
In the space of letting go, she let it all be.
A small smile came over her face. A light breeze blew through her.
And the sun and the moon shone forevermore."
Today... Just let go...

Journaling from the soul…

Is “letting go” hard for you?
What are you hanging on to that’s holding you back in life?
Write a story about how you “just let go.”
Make a list of ways you can let go.

"Don't miss all the beautiful colors of the rainbow looking for that pot of gold."
-Unknown

Most of us need to slow down and appreciate life more...
We need to do less...
Once we do...
We are more present with the people who we are with...
We are more mindful of what we are doing...
We are more grateful... and appreciate so much more...
We understand that life is a gift... not to be taken for granted.
Today... Slow down and appreciate what you are doing...
what you have... having more awareness in each and every moment...
When you find yourself moving too fast... stressing out...
or wishing things were different...
Take a long... deep... breath (inhale slowly for 4 seconds filling up all four corners of your belly... gently hold it for 4 seconds...
and exhale slowly for 8 seconds)... Do this 3 times.
Notice how you feel... in this moment... and the next...
and the next...
Being thankful for everything...
Smiling...
enjoying your day!

Journaling from the soul…

Does life move too fast for you?
Where can you slow down?
Are you present… living in the moment?
Use your five senses and observe the space you are in right now…
What do you… See? Hear? Feel? Smell? Taste?

"People will love you as much as you love yourself. People will naturally value you as much as you value yourself."
-Yung Pueblo

When we love ourselves first… all falls into place.
Life is a mirror... and our relationships and how people treat us are a reflection of us.
If we don't love and value ourselves... we will attract people who don't love and value us.
When we learn to love ourselves more... we will feel better... attracting what we deserve into our lives... not just with relationships... but in all areas of our life.
When we are in a situation where someone is not treating us as we would like to be treated... we can ask ourselves important questions...
"Am I creating this? Is this person reflecting how I feel inside... perhaps my shadow side?
Is there something for me to learn here... are they showing me something I need to know... perhaps letting go and moving on... setting boundaries...
How can I let go of being in victim mode... blaming others for how I feel... taking responsibility and working on loving me more?"
Then when we change... and love and value ourselves more... we suddenly notice others changing around us... helping us... being kinder... becoming more!
Today... Choose to make yourself a priority...
Accept and value yourself... flaws and all...
Being kind and gentle with yourself... remembering you are a special child of God.
Empowering yourself... bringing more peace... joy... confidence... into your life each and every day!
You're worth it!

Journaling from the soul…

How do people treat you?
Are they mirroring what's inside of you?
If you want more respect… can you respect yourself more?
How can you set healthy boundaries for yourself and love yourself more?

"Your journey will be much lighter and easier if you don't carry your past with you."
-Unknown

It has been said… the more "weight" we carry from our past...
The longer we have to "wait" to live the life of our dreams.
So many people are trapped in their past... experiences from their childhoods... mistakes they think they made... grudges they carry...
what happened to them... what didn't happen...
When we are stuck in the past... it weighs us down.
When we are weighed down...
Things slow down... like attracting what we want into our lives...
or healing.
Because our energy goes to the past not the present.
Today... Let go... forgive... give up trying to know
why things happened the way they did...
Live in the moment... surrendering... trusting that what has happened in your life... was created for the best possible reasons.
Love who you are today... love where you are... being grateful...
while dreaming about the future!

Journaling from the soul…

What are you carrying from your past?
Is it heavy?
What has it done to your body… physically?
How are you going to release it… and let it go?

"All flowers must grow through dirt." -Unknown

Life is a journey…
We all have struggles and problems to solve.
Our lives ebb and flow...
If life was perfect... we wouldn't be here on planet earth.
We all have lessons to learn... making us stronger.
We came here to learn... grow... and evolve...
Our pasts are never a mistake... especially when we learn from them.
Our struggles offer gifts... when we are ready to see them...
learning what we want in life... learning what we don't want...
learning patience... acceptance... and how to love more.
Today... Keep your head up high... stay strong... fully taking in your life experiences... the good... the bad... and everything in between...
Being grateful for the wisdom you are obtaining... and the gifts...
Continuing to look for all the miracles in life... being positive...
having faith all is meant to be... loving life right now in this moment!

Journaling from the soul…

What have you had to go through… to get where you wanted in the past?
Are you experiencing any difficulties now?
Are you learning anything?
Write about the gifts you have received in the past…
And the gifts you are receiving right now.

"Yesterday is history.
Tomorrow is a mystery.
But today is a gift...
That's why we call it the present."
-Master Oogway, Kung fu panda

Life is a gift.
Today is a great day...
Can you feel it?
We are collectively feeling lighter... clearer...
and have more will and strength to change our lives for the better.
Some of us have been on auto pilot... out of our bodies...
letting our ego call the shots...
Taking life for granted... not feeling appreciation
for this life we have...
this body we have... and all our amazing gifts
we have come here to share...
We are slowly "waking up" and wanting more... a deeper connection with our Higher Selves... with God... with others...
We are craving purpose... harmony... peace... balance... and desire to be in the moment more... appreciating every moment of our lives...
living life to the fullest.
Today... Take a deep breath in...
giving thanks for another day...
the greatest gift we can receive...
setting an intention to be kind to yourself...
and do one thing that will positively change your life for the better...
because you're worth it!

Journaling from the soul…

Have you been on "auto pilot?"
What could you do differently to take care of yourself…
Physically… mentally… emotionally… spiritually?
Do you feel a shift happening… waking up and wanting more?
How can you add more peace… harmony… balance… purpose…
into your life?

"When I was 5 years old, my mother always told me that happiness was the key to life. When I went to school, they asked me what I wanted to be when I grew up. I wrote down 'happy'. They told me I didn't understand the assignment, and I told them they didn't understand life."

-John Lennon

Happiness is always available for us.
Life is about change and balance...
We have highs and lows...
Good and bad...
The key to happiness is knowing that we are all
in charge of our own happiness...
It is always there for us...
The door is always open...
We will always have a new opportunity to create our own happiness.
Today... Find something that brings you joy...
Don't let things get in the way of your happiness.
Remember... When you are happy...
You make others happy too...
Rippling out into the world.

Journaling from the soul…

Do you let others get in the way of your happiness?
Do you believe you are in charge of your own happiness?
What brings you joy… makes you happy?
Create a "dream" schedule that would make you happy.

"You don't always need a plan. Sometimes you just need to breathe, trust, let go, and see what happens."
-Mandy Hale

When we try and force "certain" things to happen...
we get in our own way.... we block what potentially
could be there for us.
It's great to get things going...
By taking some action...
yet being careful not to force anything...
being open to what evolves.
If things fall apart along the way...
it might be a sign there's something better for us.
Today... Take the action and let go of the results...
trusting that what you want will show up for your highest good.
Breathe in for 5 seconds into your heart center...
softening that area... relaxing...
Audibly breathe out with your mouth open for 5 seconds letting go...
surrendering...
Repeat!

Journaling from the soul…

Have you taken action toward a goal lately?
Are you trying to force a certain outcome?
Is there room for you to let go… and see what the Universe brings you?
Where in your life could you take some action?
Write about what you want to do.

"The simple things are also the most extraordinary things,
and only the wise can see them.
-Paulo Coelho

Cherish all the simple things in life.
Life is made up of moments.
Sometimes we rush through them and miss what's right in front of us...
We don't take time to slow down and appreciate the gifts in our lives...
Children playing... extra sleep... a great conversation with a friend...
the smell after it rains... family support... a sunrise or sunset... great music...
a smile from a stranger… a long hug... a healthy body...
The simple things that make us happy and feel good.
Today... Take time and notice all that is around you...
Take it in... moment by moment...
enjoying and appreciating the simple things in life!

Journaling from the soul…

What simple things in your life do you enjoy?
Do you make time for them?
Look around… what do you see? What are you grateful for?
Write about all the simple things in your life that you appreciate.

"Think of all the beauty still left around you and be happy."
-Anne Frank

Our world is perfectly imperfect... And in every situation we have a choice...
we can find what's wrong...
or we can find all the good in our lives...
Looking past the imperfections...
Perhaps looking past...
The comments that were made... the atmosphere that wasn't just right...
the people who didn't meet our expectations...
The mind is powerful...
We will see the world as being wonderful if we choose to see it that way...
flaws and all...
If we fill our minds with positive thoughts...
our world will start to change...
Today... Choose happiness...
Look for something positive to focus on...
even if it's harder than other days...
Perhaps the lesson is learning what you prefer in life...
Trying to find the gift in all situations... feeling grateful...
feeling blessed!

Journaling from the soul…

What are you focusing on right now?
Is your mind thinking about what went “wrong?”
How can you turn that around?
Write about all the wonderful things that have happened and are happening.

"Perfectionism is a twenty-ton shield that we lug around thinking it will protect us, when, in fact, it's the thing that's really preventing us from taking flight."
-Brene Brown

Some of us are perfectionists... and some are "recovering" perfectionists...
working on freeing ourselves...
Perfectionism comes from beliefs we carry about ourselves...
and others...
Beliefs that we have picked up along the way...
We learned these beliefs when we were trying to gain love and approval...
to fit in... to be accepted... to be successful... to stay safe...
We can shift and dissolve these old limiting beliefs...
as beliefs are only thoughts that we keep thinking... again and again...
When we hold such high expectations and standards for ourselves
and others... we suffer.
We feel a lot of pain when our expectations aren't met...
we feel frustration... irritation... anger... regret... guilt... shame...
All low energies... lowering our vibe.
We have a hard time forgiving ourselves and others...
Today... Let go of rigid expectations... they are just thoughts...
Practice self compassion...
Practice love and forgiveness for yourself and others...
it's a daily practice...
We all make mistakes... all of us.
Enjoy life... enjoy others... life is meant to be fun.
Growing your wings... being free...
soaring!

Journaling from the soul…

Would you call yourself a perfectionist in any area of your life?
Do you have rigid expectations of yourself and/or others?
How has it affected your life?
How can you practice self-compassion?

"It doesn't take a lot of strength to hang on,
it takes a lot of strength to let go."
-Unknown

Sometimes we fear change... we resist it...
Our egos come up with all these reasons why we should hang on...
stay the same... staying status quo...
Even though we know what we are currently doing... is not serving us anymore...
and we know there is more... as our Higher Selves have been nudging us...
We may resist... a job change... relationship changes... diet changes...
health changes... home changes... routine changes...
We cling to the old with all our might... and we claim all the reasons
why it works for us...
And then suddenly we wake up one day... and decide...
maybe I don't need it that way after all...
maybe I can create a new way... a new habit... a new normal...
And then life starts to shift... change... and get better and better!
Today... Don't be afraid of change...
beautiful things come from change...
Pay attention to what you're resisting... what you are attached to...
what's holding you back from living your best life...
pay attention to the still small voice inside!

Journaling from the soul…

Are you going through change right now?
Are you resisting or allowing it?
Have you… in any way… asked for it?
Write a letter from your Higher Self to you…
Explaining why the change is beneficial. Don't overthink… just write…

"How people treat you is their karma: How you react is yours."
-Wayne Dyer

We have heard the phrase... what goes around comes around...
And we have probably
experienced the truth of that.
Sometimes right away... sometimes later...
Our thoughts... words... and actions... positive or negative... affect us.
The choices we make... create a chain of cause and effect...
Again... positive... or negative...
The choices to perhaps...
Gossip... be rude... treat others poorly... being unkind...
Or...
Lift others up... stand up for people... help others... being kind...
Karma can be our greatest teacher... giving us the opportunity to understand the consequences of our actions...
Today... Choose well in life...
whether you believe in karma or not...
As you are here to fulfill your highest destiny…
You came here to do great things… to learn… grow… evolve…
love… forgive…
You can always do better today than you did yesterday…
Being kind... being loving... serving and helping others...
And when you do... notice how your life changes!

Journaling from the soul…

Karma allows us to experience what it's like on the other end…
either way…
When in your life have you noticed what you put out… came back?
We can all do better than we did yesterday…
Write about the "new you" today… what do you want to change
in your life?

"When you're in a dark place, you sometimes tend to think you've been buried. Perhaps you've been planted. Bloom."
-Peenhaz Hussain

Sometimes we may feel stuck...
and we may feel as if we aren't making progress...
Yet this "stuck" feeling... might be a lovely rest on our journey...
A time to heal...
A time to cultivate strength... courage... wisdom... faith... inspiration...
Surrendering to the Divine... (it's not giving up...)
Believing... and trusting...
ALL WILL BE WELL!
Today... Have faith... all is working out...
Heading towards what you desire...
Being grateful in advance...
Continuing to go after your dreams... taking action...
Taking chances... living life... loving your life...
Having fun... making your life as interesting as you can!

Journaling from the soul…

Do you feel like you aren't making any progress?
If you feel stuck… is this break on your journey teaching you anything?
What action can you take right now?
Write a letter to yourself giving advice on how to surrender and let go.

"Everything will be ok. Trust me.
-God

We overthink and worry about a lot.
It's helpful to find peace and be okay with where life is right now...
Taking the action we need to... and letting go of the results...
Letting go of unnecessary fear... worry... and fret...
When we try to control life... we worry and have fear...
We only create more to worry about and more to fear...
magnifying the negative.
When we are hopeful and believe all will be well...
trusting life will work out...
Life unfolds naturally... and beautifully.
Today... Take a deep breath in...
Breathe in... filling up all four corners of your belly...
hold it... exhale...
let it go... letting go of anything that's not serving you anymore.
Having faith and trusting that everything will be okay...
Being positive and optimistic...
believing the best is yet to come!

Journaling from the soul…

What have you been worrying about lately?
Where in your life can you let go a little more?
Do you trust that all will be ok?
List all the ways you can relax and let go.

"The reason you want every single thing that you want in life, is because you think you will feel really good when you get there. But, if you don't feel really good on the way to there, you can't get there. You have to be satisfied with WHAT IS while you are reaching for more."

-Abraham Hicks

It's important to be happy with where we are...
while dreaming for more...
If we can enjoy the journey... being grateful... content... joyful...
we raise our vibe...
Attracting the next positive thing... and the next... and the next...
getting in the flow!
Enjoying the journey... moment by moment...
Life is all about the journey... yet we all live for the destination... the end result...
I'll be happy when...
When I lose the weight… when I get the job… when I land the deal or get the promotion… when I retire… when I meet my soul mate…
when I'm married… when I have a bigger house… when I have a smaller house…
when I have more money…
when I go on the vacation…
when I do purposeful work… when I work less… when I have friends who love and support me… when the weather is better… when I go to school… when I finish school…
when I have kids…
when my kids are older…
when my kids are happy…
Can we be happy right now?
Today... Change your perspective...
finding all the good in your life right now...
There is so much!!!!
Think of all the things you are grateful for today... feeling love and gratitude in your heart... feeling deep gratitude... and then think of all you want in your future...
it's okay to dream!
Don't forget to dream big!
Happy and satisfied now = Dreams come true!
It's a win win!!!

Journaling from the soul…

What are you wishing for right now?
I'll be happy when…
What can you do to be happy right now?
What are you grateful for in this very moment?

"Worry is a thief. It can steal your time, joy, and peace."
-Unknown

We often worry because we are unconsciously trying
to control the future...
Unfortunately... we cannot predict nor control it.
What we can do is focus on the things we can control like our thoughts... words...
and actions.
We can also set the intention and focus on today.
Letting go of negative thoughts about the future... (the what ifs..)
Enjoying life right now... in this moment.
Today... Say a prayer... asking for support and guidance...
You don't have to do everything on your own...
Have faith... trust... find peace by letting go... surrendering... being grateful...
All is well!

Journaling from the soul…

Do you spend your time worrying?
What are you worrying about right now?
Can you turn it over to God… and let go?
Write a prayer asking for guidance.

"Surround yourself with people who push you to do better. No drama or mess. Just higher goals and higher vibrations. Good times and positive energy. No jealousy or dislike. Simply bringing out the absolute best in each other."

–Unknown

It has been said… we become like the five people
who we spend the most time with…
It's important to know ourselves… to be ourselves…
and to honor ourselves…
And to evaluate what we want in life.
It's okay to be picky regarding how we spend our time.
If we commit to events that don't fill us up…
or hang with people who zap our energy…
our frequency will be drained… lowering our vibe.
Which creates and attracts more low energy things
and events coming our way.
Today… Make the choice to surround yourself with positive energy…
Hanging around people who inspire you… care about you…
love you…
and believe in you… people who make you feel good.
Committing to events that lift you up… and bring you joy!
Leading to living your best life imaginable!

Journaling from the soul…

Name the five people who influence you the most.
What are the positives and negatives you obtain
from these relationships?
Do you engage in events that don't fill you up?
What would make you happier?
Describe your "perfect tribe."

"Daring to set boundaries is about having the courage to love ourselves even when we risk disappointing others."
–Brene Brown

It's important we learn to feel comfortable setting
healthy boundaries for ourselves.
Boundaries are key to living a healthy and happy life.
We can't be everything to everyone… it will drain us.
We don't have to put ourselves in situations that take our energy…
we have a choice…
When we set boundaries… at first we might feel uncomfortable… guilty…
awkward… or even selfish… we need to set them anyway.
Others might be surprised…
But they will actually feel better when we do…
as people crave healthy boundaries…
Setting a clear boundary is a measure of self-esteem…
showing we value ourselves… loving ourselves enough to do what we want…
doing what feels right to us…
It's time to take care of ourselves!
Today… Think about an area in your life where you give too much…
take too much… don't honor yourself…
Make a shift… setting a clear boundary…
making you a priority…
Starting small… being strong…
It's time to live the life you dream of living… with more peace…
joy… freedom…
and love!

Journaling from the soul…

Are you good at setting boundaries for yourself?
Where do you need to set boundaries?
How can you make yourself a priority?
What can you let go of that will make you happier?

"I am unique. I am special. I am love. I am me. I am..."
–Unknown

I am... two powerful words... what we put after them... creates our destiny.
We can all be more aware of what we create and manifest...
Abraham Hicks wrote... "When you say, "I am," the words that follow are summoning creation with mighty force,
because you are declaring it to be fact.
You are stating it with a mighty force. You are stating it with certainty.
And so immediately after you say, "I am tired" or "I am broke" or "I am sick" or "I am late" or I am overweight" or "I am old,"
the Universe says, "Your wish is my command.'"
Today... Be mindful... paying attention to the words that you speak...
I am... two very powerful words...
I am... a holy expression... (I am that I am... God...)
I am... words we use to define who we are...
Making a shift...
Instead saying...
I am beautiful... I am open to all possibilities... I am inspired...
I am grace... I am love... I am compassionate... I am strong...
I am enough...
I am peace... I am joy... I am smart... I am happy... I am adventurous...
I am blessed...
I am grateful!!!!

Journaling from the soul…

What do you habitually say? I am…?
What does "I am" mean to you?
Make a list of positive "I am" statements…
Don't overthink… just write from the heart…

"A thought is harmless unless we believe it. It's not our thoughts, but our attachments to our thoughts, that causes suffering. Attaching to a thought means believing that it's true, without inquiring."
-Byron Katie

It's amazing to think that our thoughts aren't always true...
When our thoughts are painful...
we link that to our lives being painful.
It's just a thought...
When in fact... in that very moment of the painful thought...
our lives were probably pretty good...
Byron Katie... an enlightened spiritual teacher...
teaches a great method to use in the moment of a negative thought...
Her book... Loving What Is... explains this further...
For example... "He never loved me."
Ask...
Is it true? (Never?)
Can you absolutely know it's true? (Is this your perception?)
How do you react when you believe that thought?
(Feel hurt... sad... less than... not enough...)
Who would you be without the thought?
(Happier... feel loved... valued...)
Turn it around... (I didn't love me...)
People who do this work eventually start to understand the power of our thoughts and feel better... feeling happier... less stressed...
more peaceful... more love.
Today... Pay attention to your thoughts...
don't assume just because they are in your head... they are true...
Work on changing your thoughts to be more loving and supporting.
It's a practice...
Affirmation for today... "I love my life... I deserve to be happy...
I'm here to THRIVE not just survive...
I believe in me!"

Journaling from the soul…

What's bothering you right now?
Is it true?
How do you react when you believe that thought?
Who would you be without that thought? (Describe yourself…)
Turn it around…

"You demonstrate love by giving it unconditionally to yourself. And, as you do, you attract others into your life who are able to love you without conditions."
–Paul Ferrini

It's important to have a relationship with ourselves...
it changes everything.
In the book... Return to Love by Marianne Williamson...
she talks about how very few of us were raised
and taught that we're essentially good.
Very few of us were given a sense of unconditional approval, a feeling that we're precious because of what we are, not what we do.
We all have layers of conditioning... we were raised and mentored by people who were raised and mentored in the same way...
(and so on and so on)
We have been taught to worry about what others think of us...
giving away our power... letting the world determine our worth.
We will be happier... gaining more freedom... attracting healthier circumstances and relationships... when we work on
and make it a practice to love ourselves first.
Today... Just be you... love yourself as you are...
be proud of yourself and how far you have come in life...
let go of your judgmental inner critic...
Letting go of layers of conditioning... and the habit of being concerned with what others think about you... loving yourself without conditions...
as you are worth it!
Affirmations for today...
"I love and accept myself just as I am...
I'm perfectly imperfect...
I love my life...
I'm so grateful!"

Journaling from the soul…

How were you raised?
Do you love yourself unconditionally?
Do you give away your power by worrying about what others think about you?
Journal… describing your relationship with yourself…

"Dear past, thank you for the lessons. Dear future, I'm ready."
-Unknown

Everything in our past has made us the person we are today.
How can we love ourselves fully… if we dislike what has shaped us?
When we have discomfort… pain… struggles… we learn a lot in life.
Be become stronger… wiser… more compassionate… more loving…
Today… Give thanks for a beautiful life…
thanking your past for all it has given you…
Thanking it for all the wisdom…
Trying not to resist the changes you are going through…
change is healthy…
We can't manifest a new future without going through
unfamiliar change…
Remembering you are braver than you believe…
keeping your hopes up…
looking forward to a brighter future!

Journaling from the soul…

Do you regret your past?
Can you find the "gifts" in past struggles?
What about a current struggle?
Write about your future.

"Keep going. Each step may feel harder, but don't stop.
The view at the top is beautiful."
-Unknown

When life doesn't go the way we want it to go...
we easily want to give up and quit.
We may think...
"I tried it... it didn't work..."
"I'm not good at it."
"There must be something else for me." "Is it me?"
We can be more patient... as we continue down our path...
letting go of instant gratification...
instant success in what we desire...
Let go of having to know all the answers...
having to figure it out today.
Instead we can trust... perhaps believing everything happens for a reason...
and we are in the process of learning what we prefer...
and heading towards a better life.
Remembering... we are worthy of great things... all of us...
we are all worthy of great joy...
We are here not only to survive but to THRIVE!
Our time will come! It may not be where we started...
but as we patiently continue down our path... one step at a time...
we discover the next thing... and the next...
Most of the time looking back... we see why things went the way they did...
we see how life is even better than we thought
it could possibly be.
Today... Believe it will always work out...
Don't give up... life is all about "failing" and getting back up again...
When we get up... we get up stronger...
giving us more knowledge of what we want...
Going forward towards a better life...
a life worth living!

Journaling from the soul…

Where in your life can you be more patient?
Do you give up easily?
Are you afraid to fail? What does that mean to you?
Write a note from your future self thanking you for not giving up.

"Peace... it does not mean to be in a place where there is no noise, trouble, or hard work. It means to be in the midst of those things and still be calm in your heart."
–Unknown

Our work is to cultivate peace within... choosing peace...
rather than practicing stress.
When we are practicing peace... we react to life with a peaceful heart... mind... and soul...
We are calm... not bothered... or irritated when encountered
with a difficult situation or problem...
We focus on the positive... seeing possibilities...
trusting and having faith that all is meant to be and for our highest good...
believing in miracles.
Creating peace is a practice for us to develop
and continually work on...
we can work on living a more peaceful life by...
Slowing down... taking time to know ourselves better...
understanding why we attract what we attract into our lives...
Being more mindful... accepting what is... spending time in nature...
spending time alone...
Breathing deeply... de-cluttering... praying... meditating...
connecting with our Higher Selves and Source Energy...
Today... Let go of the control... the control of thinking life should be a certain way... let go of resisting WHAT IS... if it's going to rain...
let it rain! (Or snow!)
Instead... surrender and allow yourself to be led...
leading you to getting into the flow... where life feels good...
taking in one beautiful moment at a time!

Journaling from the soul…

What do you try and control?
Do you have a peaceful mind? Heart?
What can you do to have more peace?
Make a plan… of what you will add into your life…
or what you will take away.

"Comparison is the thief of joy."
-Theodore Roosevelt

When we compare... we rob ourselves of the life we could have. The life of peace... joy... freedom... inspiration... love...
We can all let go of the self-sabotaging habit
of comparing ourselves to others...
It's a habit that blocks and closes our heart centers... creating low energy... then attracting low energy people... things... events...
into our lives...
We can shift this habit by practicing being more aware of our thoughts... identifying more with our souls... being the observer of this internal critic... our egos... the "roommate" living with us...
We can eventually take our power back with continuous practice...
by noting the thought... not judging it...not identifying with it...
not believing it.
Eventually... as we become more confident...
these thoughts won't even arise...
Being truly happy for others... feeling content with where we are...
at the same time excited about creating our future!
Today... Open your heart... feel gratitude and love in your heart center...
(think about someone you love...)
Inhale... breathe into your heart center...
hold your inhale while feeling gratitude...
Exhale... (picture a flower opening...) sending love throughout your body and out to the world through your heart. Repeat...
Now... tune in...
Notice your mind... do you feel calmer... more peaceful...
Notice your body... do you feel more relaxed...
Notice your heart... do you feel it opening...
feeling love...

Journaling from the soul…

Watch your thoughts for a while… what do you hear?
When you're with others do you compare yourself to them?
Do you keep your heart open or closed?
Close your eyes… open your heart… notice how you feel…
what do you see?
Hear… know… and then write about it.

"The secret for health for both the mind and body is not to mourn for the past, not to worry about the future, nor to anticipate troubles, but to live in the present moment wisely and earnestly."

–Buddha

We live mostly in the past or the future… and unfortunately it drains our energy… causing suffering…
Living in the present can be difficult to learn… but we can work on it… and achieve it more and more.
We can all learn to slow down… and "stop and smell the roses"…
And appreciate our lives where we are today… right here and now in this moment… and the next… and the next…
"Being satisfied with what is… and excited about what's to come!"
Tuning into and appreciating all we sense… what we see… feel… hear… taste… smell…
Being more aware… breathing into our heart centers…
feeling immense gratitude for life and those in our lives!
Today… Let go of regrets from the past…
it's not worth hanging onto what might hold us back…
and let go of fearing the future…
Try and live in the moment… living in the now…
Developing the attitude of gratitude… feeling grateful…
and expressing that gratitude to other people…
saying "thank you"…
The more gratitude…
the happier your life will be!

Journaling from the soul…

Do you spend most of your time thinking about the past and the future?
Does it drain your energy?
How can you live more in the moment?
Focus on what you appreciate right now… feeling gratitude in your heart.

"If you correct your mind, the rest of your life will fall into place."
-Lao Tzu

Our minds are so powerful…
Sometimes convincing us everything is wrong…
Our minds can either limit us… or can empower us...
depending on what we allow…
We can train our minds…
We can learn to quiet our minds/egos… checking in with our Higher Selves…
our intuition… listening to our soul speak.
Wayne Dyer often explained… EGO – Stands for… Edging God Out…
Today… When your mind starts to report what's wrong… take a deep breath
in… connecting with your heart center… spirit… exhale…
quieting your mind… feeling love… joy… and gratitude!
Today's Affirmations...
"I am so grateful…
I feel so blessed…
I love ______…"

Journaling from the soul…

Do you live mostly coming from your E.G.O.?
(Edging God Out?)
Does your mind focus on what's wrong more than what's right?
Make a list of all the things you love in life.

"First, it is an intention.
Then a behavior.
Then a habit.
Then a practice.
Then a second nature.
Then it's simply who you are."
-Brandon Burchard

Knowledge is important...
but unless we put what we learn to practice...
it won't stick.
We learn all the time... we listen... we read all these great ideas on how to change our lives...
They make sense and we intellectually know what to do...
Unfortunately... unless we take action... changing our behavior...
nothing will change...
We can start with setting an intention... naming what we want...
getting a clear picture... feeling it...
Then we can take action... towards what we want...doing something...
again and again... (this is where we get stuck... we try eating a different way...
meditating... moving our bodies... etc...
and then we say... I'm not good at it... and stop...)
Soon it becomes a habit... an action we do regularly...
without little thought...
Then a practice... after we've done it so much...
it becomes automatic...
Then second nature... done easily...
Finally, it's who we are... we are it... and it is us...
And our lives transform and shift... and we grow and evolve!
Today... It's time to take action towards what you want in life...
and keep going... not quitting even if it feels uncomfortable at first...
It takes time to develop a practice eventually becoming you...
your life...
the new you!

Journaling from the soul…

What are you longing for right now? Set the intention.
How can you make it a habit or practice?
What action can you take?
When things get hard… what can you do to keep going?
What would the "new you" be like if you reached your goal?

"It's difficult to find the leverage to make a difference. At your job, there are probably people with more experience than you, who have more domain knowledge than you, even more skills than you. The same is true about your competition. But there's one place where you can make your mark: Your attitude. You can bring more generosity of spirit, more enthusiasm, more kindness, more resilience, more positive energy, more bravery and more magic to the room than anyone else, at least right now. Because you choose to.
That can be what you stand for."
–Seth's Blog

Our attitude in life is so important.
We can apply this idea to more than our jobs…
to all the different areas in our lives…
Today… Choose to stand out… be positive…
make a difference…
have a great attitude… changing your life…
changing the lives of others…
creating opportunities…
creating fun…
creating miracles!!!

Journaling from the soul…

Describe your current attitude in life.
Do you bring excitement… kindness… positive energy… into life?
How do you stand out?
Write about someone who you admire who does this. What are their qualities?

"If you really want to receive joy and happiness, then serve others with all your heart. Lift their burden, and your own burden will be lighter."
–Ezra Taft Benson

There is an intriguing article by Rachel Naomi Remen… she says…
"When we help… We see life as weak.
When we fix… We see life as broken
When we serve… We see life as whole.
Fixing and helping may be the work of the ego…
serving is the work of the soul. "
When we try to "fix"people… there's never a good outcome.
(We create negative karma…)
When we try and help people…
we get in the way of their own personal growth.
When we serve… there is a relationship between equals.
Simple ways to serve…
Smile at others… hold the door for someone…
share your dreams and inspiration with someone…
listen deeply to a conversation…
care about others… volunteer…
Give someone a compliment… buy lunch for a person in need…
teach someone how to do something…
check in on someone who needs it…
Give a caring hug to someone who is hurting… encourage others…
Today… Serve others… using your God-given talents…
one person at a time… feeling more joy and happiness…
Spreading light and love!

Journaling from the soul…

Do you help… fix… or serve?
What do you want to change?
What can you do for other people?
What are your gifts/talents that you can spread around the world?

"If you truly loved yourself, you could never hurt another."
-Buddha

This quote is deep… bringing many questions and interpretations…
One of the most important things we can do in our lives…
is cultivate self-love…
When we love ourselves… what's inside of us… shines out onto others…
as we are all one…
When we love ourselves…
we see the reflection of that love within someone…
As they reflect back to us what's inside of us…
Being human… being imperfect… it's totally possible we will get hurt…
and hurt others… (which we may do without even knowing)…
What we can always be aware of and work on is coming from a place of LOVE…
doing the best we can… loving ourselves as much as we can…
working towards unconditional love… towards ourselves…
and then others!
Today… Love yourself… take care of you… say no when you need to…
value your time and value your feelings and needs…
That's where it all starts!
When you do… when you make yourself a priority…
your life will start to change…
one day at a time!

Journaling from the soul…

Thinking back… have you knowingly or unknowingly hurt other people?
Was it related to how you felt inside?
Have others hurt you? Can you see why they may have done it?
Continue to write… see what comes up for you.

"Jealousy is a common feeling and usually stems from a place of lack in our lives."
–Unknown

We have all felt jealousy towards someone or something…
Jealousy can be a normal… programmed… a go-to… emotion we feel.
Unfortunately… it is a low vibrational emotion.
Why are we jealous?
Possibly… lack of self-love… feeling unworthy of having things…
maybe we live in fear and scarcity mode
believing there's not enough for everyone.
And when we are in the state of jealousy… we lower our vibration and attract lower vibrational people and events into our lives…
as well as more things to be jealous of… or people jealous of us.
Abraham Hicks talks about an emotional guidance scale…
rating emotions from highest vibration to lowest…
and jealousy is way on the bottom of the scale…
Today… Examine your emotions of jealousy… note when you feel it…
name it… allow yourself to feel it without judging yourself…
and allow it to pass through… remembering emotions are energy…
they can come and go… we just don't want to stuff them…
Let it go… and allow a higher vibration to flow into your life…
you're worth it… working your way up the scale…
Set an intention to live your life mostly towards the top of the scale…
being positive… having passion… feeling joy… love… freedom… inspiration…
living your best life possible!
And watch your life change!

Journaling from the soul…

Who triggers jealousy in you?
What do they do? What are they like?
Are you more jealous at certain times? Maybe when you have low energy?
What lifts your energy… make a list…
Commit to making it your daily practice.

"The more I love and value myself, the more I allow positive things to come into my life. The less I love myself, the less I feel worthy of allowing positive things to come into my life."
–Anita Moorjani

Loving ourselves doesn't always come easy…
it's a practice we can all cultivate and work on…
It actually might feel foreign at first…
as we may have been conditioned to believe it's wrong or selfish…
When we feel hurt… sadness… frustration…
because we feel others may be taken advantage of us… not respecting us…
not valuing us… not loving us…
We might tune in and ask…
Is it possible they are mirroring back what's inside us?
Or what needs to change?
Loving ourselves is so important!
The more we love ourselves… and value ourselves…
The more our lives will take off… changing for the better…
We will feel better physically… our bodies will heal… we will feel better mentally… letting go of unnecessary mental chatter…
anxiety and stress… we will feel better emotionally… spiritually…
Our relationships will improve and will be more harmonious…
We will feel more comfortable being alone…
or not included (ending FOMO-fear of missing out)…
New and exciting opportunities will appear in our lives!
Today… Take time to love and accept yourself…
where you are right now…
Journal about what you like about yourself…
focusing on all your amazing gifts and strengths….
letting go of what doesn't serve you…
Focus on you… loving you first…
instead of other people loving you…
and watch your life transform!

Journaling from the soul...

What do you like about yourself?
What gifts/strengths do you have?
What can you release that doesn't serve you any longer?
What can you do to love yourself more... focus on that!

"If you don't believe in miracles...
perhaps you've forgotten you are one."
–Unknown

Believe... in... miracles...
Miracles happen all the time…
We all can agree there's more going on in our world that just what our physical eyes can see…
It's important to always believe… even if it doesn't seem possible…
When we believe with all our heart…
we open up to receiving more miraculous outcomes…
It's our faith and belief that attracts the magic in…
Today… Believe in miracles…
believe in infinite possibilities… believe in prayer…
believe in a Higher Power greater than you… when you do…
magic happens!
If you have been struggling… surrender… handing it over to Source…
to your Angels… trusting all is well and meant to be! And so it is!
Affirmation for today…
"I surrender… and let go… I am here… and all is well…"

Journaling from the soul…

What are you going through in your life right now?
Could you use a miracle?
Write a prayer requesting a miracle.
Read it out loud.

"Anything you can't control, is teaching you how to let go."
-Jackson Kiddard

Our work is to be less attached...
We all have times when we are attached to certain outcomes...
Sometimes we try and control our outcomes too much...
even trying to controlling others' outcomes...
We can learn to let go...
Letting go of holding on so tightly... when we try and control...
we feel fear... worry... anxious... all low energies...
which attracts low vibrational situations into our lives.
As we let go... we actually get closer to what we want...
as we aren't getting in the way...
We let go of forcing things to happen... and we believe when it's the right time...
it will come to us... without much effort... being patient...
We can take action towards what we desire... exploring opportunities when they appear... getting into the flow... leading to great things...
Doing the work... and then letting go... surrendering to the Divine...
Today... Let go... let your heart lead the way...
dissolving any unhealthy attachments in your life...
accepting life the way it is right now...
in this moment... and the next...
Opening up to "what is"...
being okay with not knowing everything...
embracing your life...
one day at a time!

Journaling from the soul...

What are you attached to?
What in your life would be hard to lose?
Is it possible to not have attachments?
What could you be less attached to?

"Twelve years from now, your future self is going to thank you for something you did today, for an asset you began to build, a habit you formed, a seed you planted. Even if you're not sure of where it will lead, today's the day to begin."

–Seth's Blog

Today is a great day to do something new.
We sometimes wait for the "perfect time"…
We have an "all or nothing" mentality…
What we really need to do… is just start…
If we are changing something or adding something to make our lives better…
it may be helpful to focus on just one thing…
Let's say we want to lose weight… find a new job…
have better relationships… make more money… etc…
We would pick ONE to focus on… doing something every day…
creating a habit… a lifestyle… a new way of being…
And all the rest will fall into place as well… as we make that one change…
and another… and another…
As we make these shifts… our vibration goes up…
and we start to attract all the amazing things we desire!
Today… Make a commitment to start something new…
believing you can do it…
Make a plan… creating a strategy… leading to the results you want…
YOU CAN DO IT! Anything is possible with a strong desire!
Starting to live the life you dream about… loving your life… now…
and years to come!

Journaling from the soul…

Is there something you want in life? Have you started to take action?
Pick one area in your life that you would like to make a change.
Write about how it would make you feel if you had this change.
Now brainstorm all the ways you can make this your reality.
Take one step today.

"Be happy for what you have while working towards what you want."
–Helen Keller

When we let go of what we think life is supposed to look like…
we benefit.
Life is a gift. We can give thanks.
Celebrating the little things we have done…
Celebrating how far we have come… (we have all shifted immensely!)
Celebrating who we have become…
Celebrating the life we have lived… with all our amazing memories…
Celebrating our family… friends… love… adventures…
fun… miracles…
Today… Make it a goal to celebrate your life… all of it…
all the beautiful things in your life…
Cherishing every moment…
Being grateful for what is… being in the moment…
while striving forward…
towards your awesome future!
Your future looks bright!

Journaling from the soul…

Today it's time to celebrate… what are you proud of…
What have you accomplished in your life?
What are you happy about today?
What are you grateful for?

"The secret of change is to focus all of your energy, not on fighting the old, but on building the new."

–Socrates

We can always change the direction of our lives.
Change is inevitable…
Yet we fear change.
Sometimes things shift… or we change our minds…
It takes courage to change direction in life…
It takes courage to listen to our hearts…
It's helpful to focus on what we want…
rather than what we don't want…
When we focus on what we don't want… rethinking the past…
spinning on what went wrong… what's going wrong…
what didn't work… what isn't working… we suffer.
Living in our heads… living in the assumption box…
making a lot of assumptions…
(When we make assumptions… more often than not…
they are not even true… affecting our peace… joy… health…)
Today… Ask yourself some important questions…
what do you want in life… how would it look…
how would it feel… who would you be with…
what do you love doing… what lights you up…
what would your dream life look like… why can't you have it?
Make an effort to move towards it… one step at a time… with curiosity…
faith… confidence… ease… grace… humility…
living your best life!

Journaling from the soul…

What do you want in life?
How would it look? Feel? Who would you be with?
What do you love doing? What lights you up?
What would your dream life look like?

"Health does not always come from medicine. Most of the time it comes from peace of mind, peace in the heart, peace of soul. It comes from laughter and love."
–Unknown

Having a peaceful mind is so important.
When we are stressed… and we worry…
we cause harm to our bodies… and to our minds.
When we don't value ourselves… not loving ourselves…
not loving who we are today…
we create pain and illness in our bodies.
When we hang on to old hurts… not forgiving… holding resentment…
we harm ourselves physically… mentally… emotionally… spiritually.
We can cultivate better overall health by working on having more peace in our lives… peace of mind… heart… and soul…
Breathing intentionally helps… doing regular…. deep and conscious breath work… taking full breaths… using your diaphragm…
Feeling grateful for life… feeling it in our hearts…
Slowing down… starting a meditation practice will change our lives …
Meditating on the phrases… the affirmations… over and over…
I am love… I am peace…
May I be happy and well…
Slowly…
Inhale… "I am love."
Exhale... "I am peace."
Inhale… "May I be…"
Exhale... "happy and well."
Repeat…
Today… Set peace of mind… peace in the heart… peace of soul…
as your highest goal…
When you do… you will feel a shift… shifting to more…
joy… love… and freedom!

Journaling from the soul…

What do you stress about?
Does it affect you physically? Emotionally? Mentally? Spiritually?
What can you do to have peace in your mind?
Peace in your heart?

"Talking about all our problems is our greatest addiction.
Break the habit. Talk about your joys."
–Rita Schiano

Complaining is one of the worst things we can do for our health…
life… wealth…
Unfortunately… most people don't even know they are doing it.
If we truly believed in the law of attraction… what we think…
say… feel…
or do… will attract the same into our lives…
We would try to be more aware of what we are putting out there.
Complaining about our bodies… our ailments… our day…
what's happening around us… the people in our lives… the traffic…
the weather… our jobs… our future…
(all habit!) only creates more to complain about.
It's a viscous cycle.
Today… Pay attention to your language…
Whether you think it or speak it.
Try and change your thoughts and words to things that are positive.
Finding all the things you love about your life.
Thanking your body for all it has done for you…
praising the people in your life… being appreciative for your job…
it will create more to be thankful for.
It might feel strange at first… but over time it will become your new habit once you see how it changes your life.
Challenge yourself to go 24 hours without complaining…
being conscious of what you are creating in your future…
you deserve so much more!

Journaling from the soul...

Do you complain a lot? What about?
Do you pay attention to the words you speak?
What would you like to shift?
Name what you love about your body... your significant other...
your friends... your job... your family... your life...

"The number one cause of unconsciousness is that we are trying to escape emotional pain. Feel it, and your health will improve."
-Eric Christopher

Emotions are energies in motion... they want to move...
We stuff our emotions... we feel fear when we have lower emotions such as worry... anger... jealousy... guilt... grief...
we try not to feel them.
We have been conditioned in society that it's not okay to show our emotions...
so we learned to push them down...
causing density in our bodies... leading to pain... suffering...
We can work through these emotions when they arise...
By breathing in deeply... and feeling the emotion that's coming up...
Being aware... perhaps asking your Higher Self for guidance...
asking what you may need to pay attention to... ask for help...
Facing the fear... being present...
Observing what sensations come up in your body...
rather than pushing them away...
Keeping your full attention on the body...
no attention on the thought...
and the emotion eventually goes away...
Today... Be aware... notice... breathe in... feel...
breathe in again...
exhale... release and let go...
Allowing the energy to pass... taking what you need to know...
healing and moving toward your best healthy self!
Affirmation you can repeat... from Louise Hay...
"All is well...
Everything is working out for my highest good...
Out of this experience only good will come...
I am safe..."

Journaling from the soul...

What emotions are you trying to stuff?
Have you pushed down emotions in the past?
Breathe deeply… what emotion do you feel?
What old wounds and trauma would you like to heal?

"It's a wonderful day. I've never seen this one before."
-Maya Angelou

Every day is another day to be thankful.
Grateful for another day on this planet… another day of opportunity…
fun… peace… love… joy…
As we know… the more grateful we are… the better our lives go…
Lifting our vibration up higher… attracting more high vibe people… things…
events… into our lives.
Unfortunately… sometimes we do the opposite…
and being grateful is not our go-to…
We try for a while and then go back to old patterns…
focusing on the worry… the negative… the what ifs… our problems…
Today… It's your choice… how are you going to go forward with your day…
your week… the next month… year?
Hopefully with the attitude of "It's a wonderful day…
one you haven't seen before"…
Believing in miracles… having faith and hope…
living your best life!

Journaling from the soul…

What is your go-to attitude in life?
Do you feel grateful?
Do you express it to others?
Make a list of everything you are thankful for…
and list what's going "right" in your life.

Made in the USA
Middletown, DE
19 January 2020

83323813R00130